"There are very few real *racers* in the world, as opposed to mere racing drivers."

–STIRLING MOSS

REAL RACERS

FORMULA 1 IN THE 1950s AND 1960s: A DRIVER'S PERSPECTIVE

Photography from The Klemantaski Collection

STUART CODLING

Foreword by David Coulthard • Afterword by Darren Heath

First published in 2011 by MBI Publishing Company and Motorbooks, an imprint of MBI Publishing Company, 400 First Avenue North, Suite 300, Minneapolis, MN 55401 USA

Library of Congress Cataloging-in-Publication Data

Codling, Stuart, 1972-
    Real racers : Formula 1 in the 1950s and 1960s : a driver's perspective : rare and classic images from the Klemantaski Collection / Stuart Codling.
        p. cm.
    Includes bibliographical references and index.
    ISBN 978-0-7603-3891-9 (hb w/ jkt)
    1. Grand Prix racing—History—20th century—Pictorial works. 2. Formula One automobiles—History—20th century—Pictorial works. 3. Automobile racing drivers—History—20th century—Pictorial works. I. Klemantaski Collection (Stamford, Conn.) II. Title.
    GV1029.15.C64 2011
    796.72'09045—dc22

                                        2010036383

Editor: Jeffrey Zuehlke
Design Manager: Kou Lor
Designed by Cindy Samargia Laun
Cover designed by Rob Johnson, Toprotype, Inc.

Printed in China

*Dedicated to those
who did not make it,
and to those who did*

ACKNOWLEDGMENTS

Thanks to everyone who has helped to bring this project together: Peter Sachs for his enthusiastic curation of The Klemantaski Collection; my editor, Jeff Zuehlke, for his patience (sorely tested) and good humor (ditto) throughout; and the editor and publisher of *Autosport* for permission to quote from the magazine's archive. Thanks also to the drivers of the period who kindly gave their time, and to the people who facilitated the interviews: David and Margaret Brabham, Patrick Crew, Silvia Hoffer-Frangipane, Derek Redfern and Sharon Bowness; to Lady Moss for a warming cup of tea on a freezing January morning, and to Emma Sekuless and Kevin Bradley of the National Library of Australia's Oral History Project. No work of research is complete without a visit to the LAT Archive under the stewardship of Kevin Wood, who as ever was kind enough to reserve the Jim Clark mug. Special thanks to my wife, Julie, for her patience and support.

—*Stuart Codling, Fall 2010*

On the front cover: Jackie Stewart on his way to victory in the BRM 61/2 at the 1966 Monaco Grand Prix. *Photo by Ami Guichard*

On the back cover: Juan Manuel Fangio testing the V-12 Maserati 250F during practice for the 1957 Monaco Grand Prix. He will revert to the straight six for the race. *Photo by Louis Klemantaski*

On the frontispiece: Stirling Moss at speed down the harbor front in the Rob Walker Lotus 18, on his way to victory at the 1961 Monaco Grand Prix. *Photo by Louis Klemantaski*

On page 2: The scene before the start of the 1957 Pescara Grand Prix, with Juan Manuel Fangio's pole-winning Maserati 250F in the foreground. *Photo by Edward Eves*

On page 208: Raymond "Toto" Roche casts Peter Coltrin a rather disapproving glance as he prepares to wave the checkered flag to 1960 French Grand Prix winner Jack Brabham. The BRM in the background belongs to Graham Hill, who dropped out of the race after a first-lap crash. *Photo by Peter Coltrin*

CONTENTS

FOREWORD

At the beginning of the 2010 Formula 1 season I was given the opportunity to drive one of the Mercedes-Benz W196s that Juan Manuel Fangio used to clinch the F1 World Championship in 1954 and 1955. What was it like to drive? I couldn't really tell you—not properly, anyway.

We were at the Bahrain International Circuit, a lavish clean-sheet facility with smoothly graded asphalt and acres of run-off, designed by a professional architect to comply with internationally agreed standards of excellence. On a gentle canter around a track like this you can only imagine what it must have been like to stretch the W196 to its limits on the circuits of the 1950s, many of which were based around public roads where the scenery was a lot closer.

Imagine what it would be like for Fangio, sitting high and exposed in the "streamliner" version of this pendulous front-engined beast, with its swing-axle rear suspension and skinny tires, bearing down on Gueux corner at Reims at over 155 miles per hour—and making the judgment on whether he could take the corner "flat"

not by consulting sheets of data, but by glancing at the trees to see how hard the wind was blowing. Daunting and risky, yes, but an irresistible challenge for any serious racing driver.

It's moments like this when you feel conflicted: You know that what you're about to do is supremely risky, but because of that very risk you've never felt more alive.

My old boss, Sir Frank Williams, says in this book that he never yearns for the "good old days." That's true enough. During my career I enjoyed the benefits of decades of scientific progress—great advances in performance and in safety, both inside and outside the cockpit—and yet still people were occasionally injured or even killed.

Driving a Formula 1 car is still the ultimate thrill. The superb photographs from The Klemantaski Collection in this book evoke an era when those thrills more often bore the risk of the ultimate price. The drivers of the day weren't foolhardy; they knew the risks. That's why, then as now, they did what they did.

—David Coulthard, Fall 2010

◀ David Coulthard takes Juan Manuel Fangio's open-wheel version of the Mercedes-Benz W196 through its paces during the Bahrain Grand Prix weekend in March, 2010. The sport has come a long way in the last half-century. *Photo © Sutton Motorsports/ZUMApress.com*

INTRODUCTION

"I never even think about the possibility that I'm not going to win."

–GRAHAM HILL

◀ Petrol and sheet steel are still rationed in the U.K. when Silverstone, a former airfield, hosts the first Formula 1 World Championship Grand Prix in May 1950, watched by several members of the British royal family. "The noise and smoke took the Queen a trifle unawares, as the mass-start of a race does to those close to the course," reports *The Motor.* That one of Alfa Romeo's prewar 158s will emerge victorious is never in doubt; the question is which one. Here Giuseppe Farina, demonstrating his distinctive laid-back driving position, commands his 300-horsepower beast with regal hauteur. *Photo by Alan R. Smith*

Driven, focused, relentless, obsessively competitive—words that aptly describe every successful modern Formula 1 driver. You could easily conjure several dozen more to describe their forebears, that hardy breed who went hurtling around makeshift courses all over the world without so much as a seat belt. And for what? Honor? Pride? Enough prize money to make it to the next race?

For those who watch and those who compete, racing is an addiction. The scenery has changed, as has the perilous balance of risk versus reward. It's now possible for a driver to retire comfortably to Monaco having banked millions, even after only a moderately successful career.

In the 1950s and 1960s the rewards were fewer, the risks greater. But for the participants, then as now, being there was often enough. Racing was all they knew, all they wanted to know, all they'd ever known. The possibility of winning, no matter how elusive, drove them on, almost without regard to their own safety. As Frank Williams says, "Once I'd started I never considered doing anything else."

Owing to the dangers involved, very few competitors from the era survive to the present day. Some of those who did survive have very kindly shared their memories for this book. Others, no longer with us, are represented by archival material. I would like to take this opportunity to thank the editor and publisher of *Autosport* for allowing me to reproduce extracts from Bruce McLaren's "From The Cockpit" column and a 1967 interview with Graham Hill. Thanks also to the National Library of Australia for granting permission to use material from its Oral History Project to supplement my interview with Jack Brabham.

THE PLAYERS

"I would say that all the racing drivers I know are very honest people—
they are what they are. They're honest with themselves
and I think this is due to the game we're in.

—GRAHAM HILL

◀ Jack Brabham (left) and Stirling Moss compare notes at the Nürburgring in 1961. The change to 1.5-liter engines has favored Ferrari, who were ready for the regulation change, and inconvenienced several other engine builders, most of whom had agitated against the change rather than prepare for it. Around the 14-mile Nürburgring Ferrari's Phil Hill sets a qualifying lap six seconds faster than Brabham can wring from his Cooper-Climax. Brabham will capitalize on damp conditions at the start to lead until his throttle jams, then Moss will put on one of the most majestic drives of his life to bring his privateer Lotus-Climax home 20 seconds ahead of the more powerful Ferraris. *Photo by Robert Daley*

In the early days, the Formula 1 World Championship calendar may have looked pretty thin—starting with just eight races—but throughout the 1950s and 1960s very few weekends went by without some form of racing in which the same cast of characters would assemble and perform. To take a brief slice of 1952 as an example, on June 29 Jean Behra, Harry Schell, Alberto Ascari, Giuseppe Farina, Stirling Moss, Prince Bira, Mike Hawthorn, Peter Collins, Maurice Trintignant, and several others competed in the three-hour Formula 2 Grand Prix de la Marne at Reims. A week later they were all back in action in the F1 World Championship round at Rouen-les-Essarts; and a week after that, many of them raced in the F2 Grand Prix de Sables d'Olonne at Les Sables before heading off to Silverstone for

the British Grand Prix on July 19. When Hill spoke of "the game we're in" he encapsulated the spirit of the age. It was an itinerant life, like a traveling circus.

Interviewed for this book, Stirling Moss pointed out that during his entire F1 career he probably raced against only a few hundred different people. Some lacked the financial stamina the life demanded and faded from the scene after only a few starts; others, sadly, succumbed to the sport's attendant risks and were lost before their time. A surprising number raced week in, week out, for many years—but still remain footnotes to history.

Besides the contributors, this chapter includes all those drivers who participated in a significant number of F1 World Championship Grands Prix during the period.

SIRSTIRLINGMOSS OBE

The son of a dentist, Stirling Crauford Moss arrived in motor racing just as interest in the sport was booming at the end of the 1940s. As a bright young talent his initial sorties in a mixed bag of British machinery—Jaguar, ERA, HWM, and BRM—caught the patriotic pulse of a nation struggling to come to terms with the aftermath of World War II. Even before he found success in Formula 1 he became a household name, and for many years after his retirement, motorists caught exceeding the speed limit could expect the police officer's opening gambit to be, "Who do you think you are—Stirling Moss?"

For all Moss's success across a range of motor sport disciplines, the ultimate prize—the F1 World Championship—eluded him. Or, rather, he eluded it: When his chance came, at the end of 1958, he in effect handed the title to Mike Hawthorn by defending Hawthorn from what he saw as an unfair penalty in the Moroccan Grand Prix. To win on a technicality, thanks to the misfortune of a rival, held no appeal at all.

Moss was still driving at the top of his form when he suffered a severe head injury during the Glover Trophy non-championship F1 race at Goodwood in 1962. As he tried to unlap himself from Graham Hill after a long pit stop for attention to his Lotus's troublesome Colotti gearbox, Moss's car left the road and struck an earth bank. The accident put an end to his F1 career at the age of 32.

WORLD CHAMPION IN 1959, 1960, AND 1966

I went to the New Zealand Grand Prix [in 1955] and that gave me the opportunity to meet some of the overseas drivers. I didn't really know anything about what was happening overseas at that time, and they suggested to me that I should come to Europe and get a year's experience. I thought, "Yeah, I'll do that." So I went over—but it took me 17 years to come back . . .

Jack Brabham trained as an engineer and worked on airplanes for the Royal Australian Air Force during World War II. He raced a self-built midget car before crossing paths with another engineer, Ron Tauranac, with whom he would eventually build his eponymous racing enterprise. After finding sponsorship to run a Bristol-engined Cooper chassis in road racing, Brabham fell foul of the Confederation of Australian Motor Sport, which decreed that his car had to run without decals. This prompted him to compete in New Zealand, a move that ultimately brought him to Europe and the workshop of the Cooper Car Company.

Working both as an engineer and a driver, he achieved enough success in sports cars and Formula 2 to lead Cooper's works assault on Formula 1. The combination of Cooper's nimble rear-engined chassis and the enlarged version of the Coventry-Climax engine (originally designed to pump water for firefighting applications) surprised everyone with its competitiveness. Brabham won the World Championship in 1959 and 1960. Climax were not ready for the shift to 1.5-liter engines in 1961 and a fallow period ensued, during which Brabham went into partnership with Ron Tauranac to build cars bearing his own name. The first F1 Brabham chassis appeared in 1962.

When F1 became a 3-liter formula in 1966 Brabham was ready with a bitsa engine based

AUSTRALIA, BORN 1926
126 GP STARTS, 14 WINS

SIR JACK BRABHAM AO,OBE

around an Oldsmobile block built by Repco. He had stolen a march on the opposition, most of whom had expended their energies lobbying against the change rather than finding a way to take advantage of it. He became the first driver to win a grand prix in a car carrying his own

name and added a third world title to his already considerable list of achievements. Brabham would race on until 1970, after which he finally returned to Australia. In 1972 the team was sold to a former motorcycle dealer by the name of Bernard Charles Ecclestone.

I saw an advert [after leaving the navy and passing his driving test, aged 23, in 1952] which said I could drive a racing car at Brands Hatch for five shillings a lap. I'd been driving the Morris [a 1938 Morris 8 Tourer] for six months and it was a real old banger, but it was a car. I had a quid's worth at Brands in a Cooper 500, and after those four laps I realized that this was what I wanted to do. It was the first time in my life that I'd known what I wanted to do. I was going to become a racing driver.

But I had no money. I knew nobody who had money to buy me a car to race, so I found that the only way to get a drive was to barter my services as a mechanic—not for money, but for the sake of a drive. But this wasn't easy either, because you don't find many people that hard up for a mechanic that they will let him loose with their pride and joy!

The Universal Motor Racing School [Hill's first client as a mechanic-cum-driver] went bust. The bloke went up the spout. He was paying for the car on hire purchase, apparently, and one day the snatch-back men came and took the car away. He disappeared . . . So there I was, high and dry with my new career suddenly foundering. But I found somebody else who wanted to start a school and told him I was just the fellow he was looking for, and that I'd had vast experience with racing schools. After all, I'd done four laps of Brands!

GREAT BRITAIN, 1929–1975
176 STARTS, 14 WINS

GRAHAM HILL

WORLD CHAMPION IN 1962 AND 1968

As Formula 1 expanded its reach via the medium of television during the 1960s the raffish, charming, slightly roguish Graham Hill came to epitomize the everyman view of the racing driver. He arrived at motorsport's top echelon the hard way, initially working as a mechanic and then shamelessly working every opportunity to make a connection—even if, as he alluded above, that meant being economical with the *actualité* . . .

He was also tremendously skilled and dedicated to the art of driving; under the bonhomie there lurked a steely competitor. When Lotus arrived in Formula 1 at the 1958 Monaco Grand Prix, Hill was driving the car. Success did not arrive overnight; a move to BRM was not immediately profitable, and such was the parlous state of the cars' preparation that Hill and teammate Dan Gurney threatened to go on strike in 1960 unless team owner Alfred Owen instilled some engineering rigor.

Hill won the World Championship for BRM in 1962 but eventually returned to Lotus, where he steered the team through the aftermath of Jim Clark's tragic death and took the drivers' title a second time in 1968. He was the only driver to win the World Championship, the Indianapolis 500 (in 1966), and the Le Mans 24 Hours (in 1972). Like Jack Brabham and Bruce McLaren, he founded his own team, but it was still in its infancy when Hill made the perhaps ill-advised decision to attempt to land his private plane in thick fog while returning from a test at the Paul Ricard circuit. He fell short of the runway and crash-landed on a golf course; several members of the team, including up-and-coming driver Tony Brise, were also killed in the impact.

BRUCE McLAREN

Bruce McLaren's racing career was a textbook case of success against the odds, and he left as a legacy one of the most successful racing teams of all time. In childhood he suffered from Perthes disease, a rare bone disorder that was only cured with time and treatment, and which left him with a slight limp. Nevertheless he developed a passion for cars and motor racing, fuelled by hours spent in the workshop of his parents' service station. He showed a talent for driving in hill climbs during his early teens and eventually obtained a Cooper Formula 2 chassis that he obsessively worked on, building on his instinctive grasp of hands-on engineering.

McLaren was the first recipient of a racing scholarship to Europe and found himself alongside Jack Brabham in the works Cooper team in 1959, winning the U.S. Grand Prix at Sebring at the end of the season, aged 22. After four seasons in F1 he founded Bruce McLaren Motor Racing, although the first McLaren Formula 1 chassis would not appear until 1966. This was the beginning of a remarkably busy period for the young team, shuttling between continents as McLaren and Denny Hulme combined F1 with a Can-Am campaign so successful that it became known as "The Bruce and Denny Show."

He took his fledgling marque's first F1 win in 1968, but Bruce McLaren Motor Racing would achieve the majority of its F1 success in his absence. On June 2, 1970 he was testing the latest version of the M8 Can-Am car—thoroughness of preparation was his team's maxim, and it would never make a new car when there was ample development room left in the current one—when the rear bodywork detached at speed on Goodwood's Levant Straight and McLaren plowed into an unused marshals' post.

GREAT BRITAIN, BORN 1939
99 GP STARTS, 27 WINS

SIR JACKIE STEWART OBE

WORLD CHAMPION IN 1969, 1971, AND 1973

Jackie Stewart was born into motor racing; his father owned a service station and had raced motorcycles, and his elder brother Jimmy became a racing driver. But dyslexia, undiagnosed until later in life, consigned him to the slow lane at school. He attributed much of his subsequent successes to the coping strategies he developed during his youth.

As a driver Stewart exhibited tremendous finesse and mechanical sympathy. Through his brother he was introduced to Ken Tyrrell, then running Cooper chassis in Formula 3, and he won the British F3 Championship first time out in 1964. That lubricated his path to F1 with BRM,

and it was an accident at Spa-Francorchamps at the wheel of a BRM P261 in 1966 (see Chapter 8) that came to define his contribution to F1 almost as much as the three world titles he would go on to win.

Rescued only by resourceful fellow competitors (who released him from the wreckage of his car with the aid of a toolkit borrowed from a spectator), Stewart suffered chemical burns from spilled fuel and the experience inspired him to become a tireless advocate for improved circuit safety—against verbigerative opposition from establishment figures. Even when he won the 1968 German Grand Prix at the

Nürburgring by an absurd margin in appalling conditions, he was lampooned in some quarters as a coward.

Stewart returned to Tyrrell's team and won the first of his three F1 drivers' titles in 1969 in a Matra chassis, then supported Tyrrell's decision to split with Matra and build his own car when Matra insisted on using its own (ultimately unsuccessful) V-12 engine. He won again in 1971 and 1973, but he had already made up his mind to retire from driving at the end of that season when his teammate and protégé Francois Cevert was killed during the U.S. Grand Prix at Watkins Glen.

I was a very experienced professional, knowing totally what I was doing on a bike. Then I had a couple of days testing in an Aston Martin, then a Vanwall, and then it was straight into a Formula Junior race. I did two F2 races and then F1, the last four World Championship Grands Prix of 1960. I had the speed but I didn't have any experience to go with it . . .

The list of John Surtees' achievements reads like at least two careers joined into one. By 1960, when he made his lightning transition to Formula 1 at the age of 26, he had amassed a phenomenal number of wins in motorcycle racing. He made the Isle of Man TT his own on a range of different bikes and took the 500cc world title four times with MV Agusta—the last one coming in 1960, when he was already impressing the world of F1 with his pace and composure on four wheels. He made his F1 debut with Lotus at the Monaco Grand Prix then returned for the last four rounds, finishing second to Jack Brabham at Silverstone and securing pole position at Porto. It was enough to earn him a full-time ride in 1961.

By his own admission, Surtees was no wallflower; he liked to immerse himself in the technical operation. At Ferrari, with whom he won the World Championship in 1964, he became increasingly disenchanted with the team's lack of focus on F1, and his relationship with team manager Eugenio Dragoni soured to the point that he walked out at Le Mans in 1966.

Surtees would go on to race for Honda and BRM in F1, but in 1966 he formed his own team as a side project to race in Can-Am. In 1969 it became a constructor, initially building customer Formula 5000 chassis, but then in 1970 it fielded a bespoke F1 chassis co-designed by Surtees himself. He retired from F1 as a driver in 1972 but the team continued until 1978.

**GREAT BRITAIN, BORN 1934
111 GP STARTS, 6 WINS**

JOHN SURTEES OBE

WORLD CHAMPION IN 1964

Frank Williams (left, with Piers Courage) hitch-hiked all over the U.K. to watch motor races in his youth and grew up determined to take part, plowing the income from his job as a traveling salesman into his own racing efforts. A chance encounter introduced him to a circle of other young racing drivers, as he relates:

I found myself with a racing Austin A35, which is a car nobody has ever heard of, but it had been raced by Graham Hill and I thought I'd have a go while I was still young. I didn't do very well but I met a lot of people, young guys from a fairly wealthy background. I put the A35 on its roof and one of the people who helped me out of the car was Jonathan Williams—no relation—who introduced me to Piers Courage [heir to the brewing dynasty, and the driver with whom Frank would enter F1 in a customer Brabham in 1969]. I joined that little clique, hanging on by the shirt tails. Even though they were from wealthy backgrounds, it was quite a hand-to-mouth existence, chasing the starting money. Jonathan and I slept on a beach before an F3 race in Sicily because if we'd stayed in a hotel we couldn't have afforded the ferry fare. Piers usually slept in his car, with his feet sticking out of the door.

It was a mixed-up paddock, people from all sorts of different backgrounds. There were wealthy people like Louis Stanley and the others who made BRM happen. That was a very British thing, a carry-the-flag exercise; all the others, apart from Ferrari, were just "Let's go racing."

Once I'd started I never considered doing anything else. It was a hand-to-mouth existence for young people, and it still is.

GREAT BRITAIN, BORN 1942 **SIR**FRANK**WILLIAMS** CBE

In 1966 Williams called time on his own driving career and set up a spare parts business, supporting his next project: a racing team. With his friend Piers Courage driving, Williams entered F1 in 1969 with a second-hand Brabham. Over the coming years Williams would have to come to terms with Courage's fatal accident at the Dutch Grand Prix in 1970, and persistent money troubles eventually led him to sell a majority stake in the team to Canadian magnate Walter Wolf in 1976. At the end of the year Williams departed and set up another team under his own name. By the end of the decade they were frontrunners, and would go on to become one of the most successful F1 teams of all time.

CHRIS**AMON**

ALBERTO**ASCARI**

GIANCARLO**BAGHETTI**

NEW ZEALAND, BORN 1943
96 GP STARTS

They say you make your own luck, but Chris Amon seemed to suffer a persistent sequence of manufacturing defects. He learned to drive in an Austin A40 on the family farm and entered his first Formula 1 race in 1963, at the age of 19, but despite exhibiting extraordinary pace he never managed to win a World Championship Grand Prix—on several occasions retiring from a commanding lead with trivial mechanical failures. After retiring from driving he returned to New Zealand and continued the family's sheep farming business.

ITALY, 1918–1955
32 GP STARTS, 13 WINS
WORLD CHAMPION
IN 1952 AND 1953

Ascari's father had been a successful driver with Alfa Romeo in the 1920s, but young Alberto was born at the wrong time: World War II curtailed his racing activities, and he finally started at the top level in 1948, at the age of 30. His name will forever be associated with Ferrari, with whom he won nine consecutive World Championship Grands Prix on his way to the drivers' title in 1952 and 1953. When the formula changed in 1954 he moved to Lancia, but the new D50 car was not ready until the end of the season. A week after crashing into the harbor at Monaco in 1955, he suffered a mysterious—and fatal—accident while testing a Ferrari sports car at Monza.

ITALY, 1934–1995
21 GP STARTS, 1 WIN

Born into a wealthy family, Giancarlo Baghetti usually had the pick of the best machinery on his route to Formula 1. He performed well in a loaned Ferrari in several non-championship races in 1960, and when Olivier Gendebien rejoined the Ecurie Nationale Belge project in 1961, Baghetti took over Gendebien's Ferrari in the World Championship. On his debut at Reims, on a day hot enough to melt the surface of the road, Baghetti achieved a unique feat: winning on his first time out. Thereafter his luck ran out; he joined other Ferrari defectors in the disastrous ATS team and then saw out the remainder of his career in second-string machinery, retiring after a one-off outing in a Lotus 49 at the 1967 Italian Grand Prix.

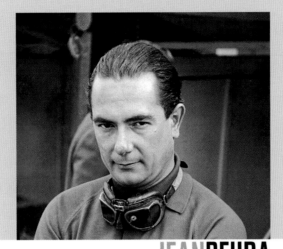

LORENZO**BANDINI**   ## JEAN**BEHRA**   ## JOAKIM**BONNIER**

ITALY, 1935–1967
42 GP STARTS, 1 WIN

Bandini had a turbulent upbringing as a result of
World War II and at the age of 15 went to work
as an apprentice mechanic. In time he started
his own business, which gave him the financial
wherewithal to indulge in his passion for motor
racing. In 1962 he came to the attention of Enzo
Ferrari and drove in three World Championship
Grands Prix, finishing third at Monaco, but he was
sidelined in 1963 and drove a BRM for Scuderia
Centro Sud in three GPs before Ferrari called him
up again to replace the injured Willy Mairesse.
He was retained as number two to John Surtees
in 1964, then found himself the team leader when
Surtees walked out in 1966. For an Italian, being
Ferrari's lead driver was a tremendous honor, but
it also brought great pressure. The burden of
expectation weighed heavily on Bandini, and in
his determination to deliver results he eventually
pushed too hard and was fatally burned in an
accident at Monaco's notorious chicane in 1967.

FRANCE, 1921–1959
52 GP STARTS

One of the greatest drivers never to win a World
Championship Grand Prix, the pugnacious Jean
Behra raced motorcycles in his native France with
some success before moving to four wheels. Like
many drivers of his era he was born at the wrong
time, robbed of several years by World War II,
and by the time he made his grand prix debut
for Gordini he was 31 years old. The cars were
underpowered, but Behra's sheer grit proved to
be a crowd-pleaser. His volatile temperament
often brought him into conflict with colleagues;
Maurice Trintignant was the first to feel the
smack of Behra's fist, but it was an ill-advised
ruckus with Ferrari team manager Romolo Tavoni
at Reims in 1959 that cost him his best drive.
Sacked on the spot, Behra entered a Formula 2
Porsche for the next GP, at Avus, and for good
measure entered the supporting sports car race
as well. It was during practice for this event that
he went over the banking and crashed, with fatal
consequences.

SWEDEN, 1930–1972
104 GP STARTS, 1 WIN

Jo Bonnier was born into a wealthy family and lived
the life of the international playboy. He arrived in
Formula 1 in 1956 as a privateer, driving rented
Maserati 250Fs. He joined BRM during 1958 and
the following year contrived to take the marque's
first World Championship win, at Zandvoort in
the previously hopeless P25. This, along with
sports car victories at Sebring and in the Targa
Florio, was the high point of his racing career. In
1961 he moved to Porsche, but the company was
unable to replicate its Formula 2 success in F1
and Bonnier's fire seemed to dwindle. He saw out
the 1960s as a privateer, often scoring respectable
top-10 finishes when the cars were reliable, but
was killed in an accident during the night at the
Le Mans 24 Hours in 1972.

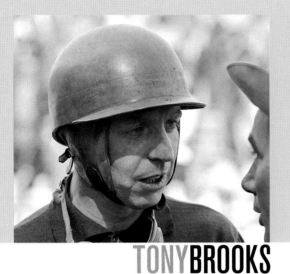

TONY**BROOKS**

EUGENIO**CASTELLOTTI**

LOUIS**CHIRON**

GREAT BRITAIN
BORN 1932
38 GP STARTS, 6 WINS
(1 SHARED)

One of the few Formula 1 drivers who can claim to have combined their studies as a dentist with a fledgling racing career, Tony Brooks enjoyed a high ratio of wins to grand prix starts. He may have won more had he not been Stirling Moss's teammate—and therefore been leaned upon to play second fiddle—at Vanwall in 1957 and 1958. When Vanwall ceased operations he signed for Ferrari, but in 1959 the front-engined cars were beginning to be eclipsed by more modern rear-engined machinery, although he was able to win at the power circuits of Reims and Avus. After disappointing seasons in 1960 and 1961 in a Cooper and a BRM, he quit racing to concentrate on building up his car dealership business.

ITALY, 1930–1957
14 GP STARTS

As a young man of 19 years Castellotti used his considerable wealth to buy himself a Ferrari, which he drove in national sports car events. He showed a natural flair for racing and came to the attention of Lancia, which gave him a drive in the Carrera Panamericana in 1953, where he impressed enough to be offered a place in the F1 program for 1954. The D50 was not ready until the end of the season, so Castellotti did not make his World Championship debut until the 1955 Argentine Grand Prix. He went on to finish second at Monaco, but Lancia's racing activities descended into chaos with the death of Alberto Ascari a week later. Enzo Ferrari bought the cars and Castellotti joined the team for 1956, but he was always a lesser priority to Juan Manuel Fangio, Peter Collins, and Luigi Musso. In March 1957 he was recalled from holiday to Modena Autodrome with instructions to beat the lap record just set by Jean Behra in the latest-specification Maserati 250F. He pushed too hard on a damp track and lost control, hitting a spectator enclosure. He was killed instantly.

MONACO, 1899–1979
15 GP STARTS

Although he started only 15 World Championship races, Louis Chiron's remarkable racing career encompassed several eras and he remained a part of the scene until his death from natural causes in 1979. Chiron's father was the maitre'd at the Hotel de Paris in Monte Carlo, and it was there that the young Chiron earned the money to go racing—he worked as a professional dance partner for wealthy ladies. He married into money and competed with great success in prewar grands prix, and after World War II he started racing again; in his elegant dress he brought the dapper style of the bygone era to the audience of the austerity years, becoming part of the elaborate tapestry that made F1 so attractive to the people. After 1953 he reduced his F1 efforts to one-off participations in his home grand prix, finally calling time in 1958 after failing to qualify. He was the driving force behind the organization of the Monaco Grand Prix for many years and particularly relished his role of waving the starting flag.

JIM**CLARK**

PETER**COLLINS**

PIERS**COURAGE**

GREAT BRITAIN, 1936–1968
72 GP STARTS, 25 WINS,
WORLD CHAMPION
IN 1963 AND 1965

Of the many superlatives often attached to Jim Clark's name, "peerless" is the most frequently and appropriately used. He was gifted with remarkable finesse, and in an era when many cars—especially the Lotuses he drove—suffered diabolical reliability, his ratio of wins to starts is genuinely astounding. His reserved persona led him to prefer the quiet life in his native Borders town of Duns, but the wealth that came with his success drove him abroad to nations with more favorable tax regimes, strictly limiting the number of days a year he could spend in the U.K. It is a sign of the esteem in which he was held that this was not greeted with the bitterness and envy the public usually directs towards tax exiles. It was almost as if he was untouchable, indestructible; so when he died, in an unexplained accident during a Formula 2 race at Hockenheim, the news was all the more shocking because it had happened to *him*.

GREAT BRITAIN, 1931–1958
32 GP STARTS, 3 WINS

It's rare for racing drivers, a fiercely individual-istic breed, to become proper friends—and yet Peter Collins is best known in the context of his relationship with Mike Hawthorn, his partner in crime during a 1957 season that passed in a torrent of good-natured practical jokes. Like Stirling Moss, Collins made his name racing in 500ccs before moving up through sports cars and Formula 2, but his final phase of maturity as a Formula 1 racer came at Ferrari in 1956, when he was partnered with Juan Manuel Fangio. It was here that he performed the other acts that have come to define history's view of him: handing his car over to Fangio unquestioningly at Monaco and Monza. At the latter race he still had a tenuous mathematical shot at the drivers' title, which he relinquished to Fangio. Hawthorn joined him for the 1957 season, and they had a thoroughly enjoy-able time, even though the car was less competitive. The 1958 246 was a better bet, but Collins lost control while chasing Tony Brooks for the lead at the Nürburgring and was thrown from his car, hitting a tree.

GREAT BRITAIN, 1942–1970
27 GP STARTS

The heir to the brewing dynasty, Piers Courage eschewed the family business and the wealth that went with it to lead a fun-packed itinerant life racing around Europe, using a shared flat in North London as a base. His racing career began in a clandestine fashion, borrowing his father's Morris Minor and racing it. His father, perhaps more wise to the goings-on than Courage believed, eventually bought him a Lotus 7 with which to go racing properly. A chance meeting with Jonathan Williams and Frank Williams led to a regular alliance, and when Courage made a mess of his first F1 break with BRM in 1967, he rebuilt his career with some exceptional performances in the Tasman series and racing for Williams in F2. When Williams moved up to F1 in 1969 with a year-old Brabham chassis, Courage demonstrated that he had shed his earlier wildness and took two second places. He turned down an offer from Ferrari for 1970 and remained with Williams, but the new De Tomaso chassis was less successful. At the Dutch Grand Prix he crashed and rolled, and the car caught fire with him trapped inside.

JUAN MANUEL FANGIO

GIUSEPPE FARINA

OLIVIER GENDEBIEN

ARGENTINA, 1911–1995
51 GP STARTS, 24 WINS
WORLD CHAMPION IN 1951, 1954, 1955, 1956, AND 1957

The self-effacing Argentine ace's top-level career lasted just a decade before he decided to retire at the age of 48. Although older than some of the people he raced against, he had tremendous stamina, a legacy of his earlier race experiences in grueling long-distance events. Out of nine Formula 1 World Championship seasons he lifted the title in five of them, and for any self-respecting manufacturer he was *the* driver to have leading the team. His last World Championship win, at the Nürburgring in 1957, at the wheel of a Maserati 250F, is widely regarded to be his greatest victory: After a slow tire change put him behind the Lancia-Ferraris of Mike Hawthorn and Peter Collins, Fangio attacked the dips and curves of the notorious 14-mile circuit with such ferocity that by his own admission he could not sleep for two days afterwards.

ITALY, 1906–1966
33 GP STARTS, 5 WINS
WORLD CHAMPION IN 1950

Born into wealth, Giuseppe Farina had the airs of an aristocrat. He raced Maseratis in the prewar era before joining Alfa Romeo, and like many of his contemporaries he lost his most competitive years to the hostilities. Returning to the Alfa Romeo fold after the war, Farina found himself cast in the unlikely role of team leader at the age of 42, following the death of Jean-Pierre Wimille in 1949. His victory in the first Formula 1 World Championship Grand Prix set the tone for 1950, but the following year his slightly younger teammate, Juan Manuel Fangio, began to assert himself and Farina only won one championship race. After the withdrawal of Alfa Romeo, he moved to Ferrari for 1952, but that was the domain of Alberto Ascari, and he took just one more win. He retired after failing to start in his final grand prix when Ferrari pulled its newly acquired Lancia D50s on safety grounds at Monza in 1955.

BELGIUM, 1924–1998
14 GP STARTS

An irregular Grand Prix entrant between 1956 and 1961, Olivier Gendebien nearly didn't make it that far after damaging himself and his car in an accident in practice for the 1955 Ulster Grand Prix at Dundrod. A tough and resourceful character, he demonstrated his appetite for danger by serving in World War II and then moving to the Belgian Congo, where he dabbled in rallying as a co-driver. Although he reached the podium only twice in World Championship F1 races, he was very successful in sports car racing, finally hanging up his helmet after winning the Le Mans 24 Hours for the fourth time in 1962.

RICHIE GINTHER

JOSE FROLIAN GONZALEZ

MASTEN GREGORY

**UNITED STATES, 1930–1989
52 GP STARTS, 1 WIN**

Paul Richard Ginther's record of one Grand Prix win undersells the achievements of a driver who was recognized by his contemporaries for his extraordinary ability to improve a car. He first emerged on the international scene after Ferrari importer Luigi Chinetti found him a seat at the 1957 12 Hours of Sebring. The Ferrari link brought him to Formula 1 for three races in 1960 (there was a fourth, for the disastrous Scarab, but he did not start). His performances earned him a full-time drive for 1961, where he dutifully supported Phil Hill to the drivers' title. Moving to BRM for 1962, Ginther played the supporting role to a different Hill—Graham—as they steered the underachieving team toward success. Honda recruited Ginther as it stepped up its F1 efforts for 1965, and he rewarded the team with its first F1 win at Mexico that year. But when the engine formula changed to 3 liters in 1966, he failed to find a competitive drive, and he quit F1 after failing to qualify the Eagle-Weslake at Monaco in 1967.

**ARGENTINA, BORN 1922
26 GP STARTS, 2 WINS**

Possibly the most unlikely looking Formula 1 driver of all time, José Froilán González was possessed of a substantial build that earned him the nickname of "The Pampas Bull." It was González who broke Alfa Romeo's stranglehold on the F1 World Championship at Silverstone in 1951, having been invited to join Ferrari to replace the injured Dorino Serafini at the previous race. Yet he remained in the shadow of his countryman, Juan Manuel Fangio. Silverstone was the venue of his second F1 victory, this time at the expense of the much-fancied Mercedes Benzes, in 1954, but the death of Onofre Marimón at the Nürburgring two weeks later disturbed González so severely that he returned to grand prix racing only irregularly after seeing out the 1954 season.

**UNITED STATES, 1932–1985
38 GP STARTS**

The young American in bottle-bottomed glasses cut an unlikely figure on the grid at Monaco when he made his Formula 1 debut in 1957. Three hours later he was the first American to finish on the podium in an F1 race—and all that in a year-old privateer car. Gregory spent his inheritance on a sports car at the age of 21 and quickly made his name racing all over the United States. By 1954 he was racing at international level and a year after that he made the first of many appearances at the Le Mans 24 Hours. But although his initial runs in F1 were impressive, in 1958 he was injured during a sports car race at Silverstone and this sapped the momentum from his single-seater career. By then the 250F was past its competitive peak and for 1959 he secured the third seat at Cooper, with Jack Brabham and Bruce McLaren. His best result was second at Porto, but then he injured himself once again in the Tourist Trophy sports car race at Goodwood, and was forced to miss the last two rounds. Cooper did not retain his services for 1960, and he never found another competitive ride, finally retiring at the end of 1965.

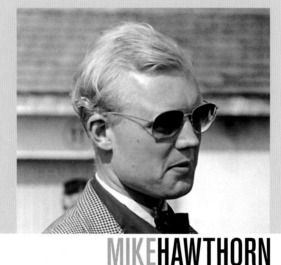

DAN**GURNEY**

MIKE**HAWTHORN**

PHIL**HILL**

UNITED STATES, BORN 1931
86 GP STARTS, 4 WINS

Another driver who combined racing talent with a gift for engineering, Dan Gurney began racing sports cars in his native California before making his first appearance at Le Mans in 1958. This led to Formula 1 tests, followed by four races in 1959. He endured a miserable year with BRM in 1960: Not only did he join Graham Hill in a threat to go on strike unless the team improved its engineering rigor, but brake failure caused him to crash, breaking his arm and killing a spectator, at the Dutch GP. Gurney's height put him at a disadvantage during the 1.5-liter era, but he took four podium finishes and a win for Porsche before it withdrew from F1. In 1964 he took Brabham's first F1 victory before following Jack Brabham's lead and building his own car for the 1966 season. The first year was not a success, largely because the new Weslake V-12 engine was not ready, but in 1967 he won the Belgian Grand Prix—a week after winning the Le Mans 24 Hours in a Ford GT40 shared with A. J. Foyt. Gurney shut down his team's F1 operations in 1968 but went on to achieve success in Indy cars and U.S. sports car racing.

GREAT BRITAIN, 1929–1959
45 GP STARTS, 3 WINS
WORLD CHAMPION IN 1958

John Michael Hawthorn brought fun and a unique sense of style to the grand prix circuit, racing in a jacket and a spotted bow tie. He came to prominence with great speed, entering his first Formula 1 Grand Prix in 1952, driving a Cooper. In 1953 he drove for Ferrari and took his first win at Reims, coolly defeating Juan Manuel Fangio in a tense slipstreaming battle. Hawthorn moved to Vanwall for 1955 and drove Jaguars in sports cars, winning the Le Mans 24 Hours; but that victory was somewhat overshadowed by the accident in which over 80 spectators were killed—and by lingering suspicions that Hawthorn had precipitated the collision. Returning to Ferrari for 1957, he teamed up with Peter Collins, with whom he had a great personal bond through their shared interest in carousing. Collins' death at the Nürburgring in 1958 marked the beginning of the end of Hawthorn's interest in motor racing; although he went on to take the drivers' title that year, he retired to look after his father's garage in Farnham. Just months later he was killed in a road accident.

UNITED STATES, 1927–2008
48 GP STARTS, 3 WINS
WORLD CHAMPION IN 1961

Like the other World Champion Hill (no relation), Phil Hill initially worked as a mechanic on other drivers' cars to create opportunities for himself. Moving to Europe, he secured a works Ferrari drive at Le Mans in 1955; three years later he hired a Maserati 250F for the 1958 French Grand Prix at Reims, just weeks after becoming the first American driver to win Le Mans. Luigi Musso's fatal accident during the course of that race created a vacancy at Ferrari, which Hill filled, but at the next race Peter Collins was also killed, leaving the young American to shoulder the burden of supporting Mike Hawthorn's title bid. This he did admirably, waving Hawthorn through to second place at the final grand prix of the year in Morocco. Hill's own Drivers' Championship came in 1961, overshadowed by the tragic death of his teammate Wolfgang von Trips. He joined the exodus from Ferrari to ATS in 1963, but the car was a failure. After 1964 he departed the F1 scene, returning twice in 1966 but failing to make the race on both occasions.

DENNY**HULME**

JACKY**ICKX**

INNES**IRELAND**

NEW ZEALAND, 1936–1992
112 GP STARTS, 8 WINS
WORLD CHAMPION IN 1967

"The Bear" began racing in hill climbs in his homeland of New Zealand, finally winning a racing scholarship to Europe in 1960. Once there, Hulme found the income to extend his stay by working in Jack Brabham's workshop, occasionally racing Brabham's sports cars and Formula Junior cars, and eventually driving with Brabham in the European F2 championship in 1964. The departure of Dan Gurney from the F1 team created a vacancy for Hulme in 1965 and he seized the opportunity to prove himself. In 1967 he hit a rich seam of form, winning the F1 World Championship with Brabham while dominating the Can-Am championship with McLaren. The following year he raced for McLaren in both series, winning the Can-Am championship, but Bruce McLaren's death in a testing accident in 1970 hit him hard. The death of his friend Peter Revson at Kyalami in 1974 proved too much, and he quit F1 at the end of the year, although he would return to action in touring cars in the 1980s.

BELGIUM, BORN 1945
114 GP STARTS, 8 WINS

Jacky Ickx arrived on the Grand Prix scene with a flourish, scoring a point in the unfancied Cooper-Maserati on his debut at Monza in 1967. He secured a seat at Ferrari in 1968 and took a thrilling victory in the wet at Rouen-les-Essarts, but a crash in practice for the Canadian Grand Prix took him out of the running for the World Championship. After a year at Brabham and two more wins he returned to Ferrari, but the team's lack of focus manifested itself in declining pace and a lack of reliability; he left after the 1973 British Grand Prix. This was a poor career move, for in 1974 Ferrari rebuilt itself around Niki Lauda, who nearly won the drivers' title, while Ickx signed for a Lotus team that was struggling to find an effective replacement for the aging 72. His F1 career fizzled out in second-string drives, but he continued to be very successful in sports car racing, winning Le Mans six times.

GREAT BRITAIN, 1930–1993
50 GP STARTS, 1 WIN

Innes Ireland's well-documented penchant for drinks and japes—largely documented, that is, by himself in his autobiography *All Arms and Elbows*—made many people view the ex-paratrooper less seriously than they ought. As one of Colin Chapman's early roster of Team Lotus drivers, he made his Formula 1 debut in the 1959 Dutch Grand Prix. Although he scored the team's first World Championship win, at the 1961 U.S. Grand Prix, Ireland was shown the door at the end of the season in favor of Trevor Taylor. He reached an agreement to drive with UDT/Laystall for 1962, and although BRM subsequently approached him, he felt honor-bound to go through with the original deal. Graham Hill, who would have been his teammate if he had gone to BRM, won the world title that year. Ireland soldiered on in second-hand machinery until 1966, then retired. He pursued a fruitful second career as a journalist.

STUART**LEWIS-EVANS**

LUIGI**MUSSO**

JOCHEN**RINDT**

GREAT BRITAIN, 1930–1958
14 GP STARTS

Lewis-Evans established his credentials in 500cc Formula 3, racing against the likes of Stirling Moss and Bernie Ecclestone, who would go on to become his manager. He joined the struggling Connaught marque for several non-championship F1 races and then made his World Championship debut at Monaco in 1957, somehow not only managing to qualify the hopelessly underpowered dinosaur but also hauling it to a fourth-place finish. Vanwall snapped him up for its third car for the rest of the season and he put it on pole at Monza. In 1958 he helped Vanwall to seal the constructors' title, but in the final race of the year his car suffered a mechanical failure and spat him off the road. He was badly burned and later died in hospital.

ITALY, 1924–1958
24 GP STARTS, 1 WIN (SHARED)

The son of a wealthy diplomat, Musso did not inherit his father's delicate touch. He is perhaps best known for refusing to hand his car over to Juan Manuel Fangio at the 1956 Italian Grand Prix, placing Fangio's title hopes in jeopardy. After Fangio defected to Maserati, Ferrari kept Musso on, but he was outpaced by Mike Hawthorn. He was pursuing Hawthorn for the lead of the 1958 French Grand Prix when he crashed, dying in hospital hours later. It subsequently emerged that Musso desperately needed the prize money to solve cashflow problems with his troubled car importing business; he also had some well-publicized gambling debts. His girlfriend, Fiamma Breschi, would later claim that Hawthorn and Peter Collins pooled their earnings but kept Musso out of the arrangement and acted together to demoralize him.

AUSTRIA, 1942–1970
60 GP STARTS, 6 WINS
WORLD CHAMPION IN 1970

Orphaned during World War II, Jochen Rindt came from wealthy stock. He did not get his hands on the family money until he reached maturity, by which time he had been sent to a private school in Chichester . . . where he developed a passion for motor sport, watching races at the nearby Goodwood circuit. He established his racing credentials by beating several leading drivers of the day in the London Trophy Formula 2 event at Crystal Palace in 1964. He took his first Formula 1 World Championship win for Lotus in 1969, and despite the troublesome genesis of the Lotus 72 car, in 1970 he had amassed a substantial championship lead by the time the F1 circus pitched up at Monza. Then tragedy struck during practice: As he applied the brakes on the approach to the Parabolica corner, something broke and his car speared off the track; the bolts securing the barrier had rusted, giving no protection from the impact. Rindt was pronounced dead on arrival at hospital, but his points lead would hold up, making him F1's first and only posthumous champion.

PEDRO**RODRIGUEZ**

HARRY**SCHELL**

JO**SIFFERT**

MEXICO, 1940–1971
54 GP STARTS, 2 WINS

Pedro and his brother Ricardo Rodriguez shone brightly but briefly on the international stage. Their father bought a Ferrari Testarossa for racing purposes, and this brought them to the attention of Ferrari importer Luigi Chinetti, owner of the North American Racing Team. Pedro was just 20 when he started at Le Mans in a NART Ferrari 250 in 1960. He lost his younger brother early, in a nonchampionship Formula 1 Grand Prix at Mexico City in 1962. Pedro did not make his World Championship debut until 1963 and took his first win aboard a Cooper-Maserati in 1967 at Kyalami. He blossomed at BRM, with whom he took his second grand prix win in 1970, and was considered one of the bravest and finest wet-weather drivers across a range of racing disciplines. He suffered a fatal accident in a Ferrari 512M sports car at the Norisring in 1971.

UNITED STATES, 1921–1960
56 GP STARTS

Harry Schell was actually born in France to racing-mad parents, who also happened to be wealthy. He grew up steeped in their racing activities, which included running Delahayes and Talbots in prewar grands prix, but at the age of 18 he lost his father in a road accident. After the war Schell lived a playboy lifestyle and was an enormously popular figure in the racing fraternity, such that everyone (except Enzo Ferrari) forgave him for cheekily short-cutting the course in qualifying at the 1959 U.S. Grand Prix. Although perhaps not the quickest driver in the field, he was competitive: His best finish was second, behind Stirling Moss, in a BRM at Zandvoort in 1958. He was attempting to qualify a Cooper at the Silverstone International Trophy in 1960 when the car skidded off the track in the wet, flipped, then hit a barrier, with fatal results.

SWITZERLAND, 1936–1971
96 GP STARTS, 2 WINS

Joseph "Seppi" Siffert is better known for his considerable sports car achievements, but he won two Formula 1 World Championship Grands Prix over the course of an eight-year career in the category. He arrived in a customer Lotus-Climax in 1962, but stepped up a gear in 1964 when he joined Rob Walker's privateer team. The environment suited him, and he was impressively competitive in Walker's second-string Lotuses, winning the British Grand Prix in 1968 against stiff opposition, most notably from Chris Amon's Ferrari. He also became a works Porsche driver in sports cars, winning several major internationals and leading its assault on the Can-Am championship. He joined fellow sports car regular Pedro Rodriguez at BRM in F1 for the 1971 season, winning at the Austrian Grand Prix, but then suffered an appalling accident at the Race of Champions at Brands Hatch when his car's suspension broke. He was trapped in the burning car and marshals were unable to extract him in time.

PIERO**TARUFFI**   MAURICE**TRINTIGNANT**   WOLFGANG**VONTRIPS**

ITALY, 1906–1988
18 GP STARTS, 1 WIN

A prewar motorcycle racer, Taruffi had dabbled in car racing and returned to the four-wheeled scene after the end of hostilities. He made his Formula 1 World Championship debut at the end of 1950 as part of Alfa Romeo's five-car entry at Monza, though he had to give his car to Juan Manuel Fangio. In 1951 and 1952 he drove for Ferrari, winning the first grand prix of 1952, at Bremgarten, then decided to focus on sports car racing, in which he was very successful. He drove in just seven more grands prix between 1953 and 1956, finishing second to Fangio at Monza in 1955 in an open-wheeled Mercedes W196.

FRANCE, 1917–2005
82 GP STARTS, 2 WINS

Another driver whose era of birth meant he lost his best years to World War II, Maurice Trintignant nevertheless enjoyed a 14-year career in the Formula 1 World Championship. His elder brother Louis suffered a fatal crash in a Bugatti Type 35 in practice for the 1933 Grand Prix de Picardie, and European power politics intervened not long after Maurice started racing in 1938. Concealing his Bugatti in a barn for the duration, Trintignant extracted the car from storage for the Coupé de la Liberation at the Bois de Boulogne in September 1945. His hurried preparations for the event resulted in one of the most unusual reasons for retirement ever given in motor racing: the fuel filter was clogged with droppings from rats that had nested in the car while it was concealed. A versatile and popular driver, Trintignant raced successfully in sports cars as well as in F1, although he never achieved team leader status in a works F1 team, which does much to explain his modest tally of wins. It is perhaps a great measure of his abilities that his two GP victories came on the unforgiving streets of Monte Carlo.

GERMANY, 1928–1961
27 GP STARTS, 2 WINS

A combination of movie star looks and raw talent provided the impetus for Wolfgang von Trips' rapid ascendance in the late 1950s, although he did not complete a full F1 season until 1960, by which time the front-engined Ferrari was outmoded. Ferrari's first clean-sheet rear-engined car was a revelation in 1961, and the young German won at Zandvoort and Aintree, arriving at the penultimate round of the season, the Italian Grand Prix, just five points behind his teammate Phil Hill, the championship leader. Von Trips put his Ferrari on pole, but dropped to fifth at the start. He was attempting to pass Jim Clark for fourth place when their wheels interlocked and von Trips was launched off the track and thrown from his car, suffering fatal injuries when he hit the ground. The car smashed into a fence and killed 14 spectators.

"Racing cars went fast and made a lovely noise. Formula 1 drivers were starting to make the newspapers. The whole thing was burgeoning."

—FRANK WILLIAMS

◄ A crowd gathers to watch one of the Lancia-Ferrari 801s being unloaded at Monte Carlo prior to the 1957 Monaco Grand Prix. Among them—dressed distinctively in a round cap, white shirt and bow tie—is Girolamo "Mino" Amorotti, Ferrari's team manager. Independently wealthy thanks to his agricultural business, Amorotti was a close friend of Enzo Ferrari and reputedly never claimed a salary from the team.

The 801 was a development of the 1955 Lancia D50 and not a tremendous success; Ferrari had been hit hard by the defection of World Champion Juan Manuel Fangio to Maserati and the deaths of Eugenio Castellotti and Alfonso de Portago. The latter's accident, in the Mille Miglia road race a week before Monaco, cost the lives of several spectators and raised the specter of criminal charges against Ferrari and tire supplier Englebert. *Photo by Edward Eves*

For a few curious years after World War II, the postwar climate of austerity coexisted uneasily with the public's growing appetite for a frivolous pursuit: motor racing. The Alfa Romeo 158 that Giuseppe Farina guided unerringly to victory in the first Formula 1 World Championship Grand Prix at Silverstone on May 13, 1950, could barely manage a handful of miles per gallon. From a pragmatic standpoint it was a spectacular irrelevance: petrol rationing would not be lifted in the U.K. for another two weeks.

Although racing rarely made the newspapers or television in the early days, it was an enthralling pursuit that generated huge crowds. Television ownership was a rare thing in itself, and to see moving images of the news one would usually have to travel to the cinema and digest a Pathé newsreel before the main feature. Motor racing was best appreciated up close, to fully appreciate the sounds as well as the sights. People would walk or hitchhike for miles to see it; and many members of the traveling circus they'd come to watch had arrived at their chosen career by a similarly tough route.

In amongst the crowds, the competitors would set up. The modern, security-gated paddock environment was a long way off. For most entrants, it was a tough existence: permanently on the road, chasing the starting money from one race promoter to the next. And yet there was tremendous camaraderie; they were all in it together, and they would have it no other way.

STIRLING MOSS

The way it worked was that the race promoters would contact the team—John Heath in the case of HWM—and ask if they'd like to enter a car. Then the negotiations would begin about how much money it would take to get there, and that was your starting money. John would often bring an extra car for a local driver, such as Rudi Fischer, because he'd get more money that way. And of course, the sums involved would very much depend on the "box office" appeal of each driver. I was lucky because I was very young, which was unusual, and to begin with we were the only British car racing. It was very useful publicity.

For my first year, with HWM, I got 25 percent of the starting money; then it went up to 33 percent, and eventually I got 50 percent.

◀ The Alfa Romeo team prepares for the first ever Formula 1 World Championship race at Silverstone. Petrol is still rationed in the U.K., and the team will have had to drive its cars, spares, and personnel across Europe (including a perilous route through the Alps) in those rickety trucks seen in the background. The 158s will be driven by Reg Parnell (4), Luigi Fagioli (3), Giuseppe Farina (2), and Juan Manuel Fangio (1). *Photo by Louis Klemantaski*

STIRLING MOSS

My first transporter was a horse box with the central divider taken out. I could just about get my 500cc Cooper in there. When I drove for HWM, their transporter was a converted bus. Later on, when I got the Maserati [250F], I used my rallying connections with the Rootes Group to get hold of a Commer van. I just rang up and said, "Can't you fix me up with a truck?" And they did. It was a very simple panel van but it did the job. What you have to remember is that when I started racing, the war had only just finished and petrol was still rationed. When that ended we were able to start going abroad.

◀ Illustrating the camaraderie in motor racing, even between rivals, brake suppliers Ferodo and Girling set their spares vans next to one another at Spa-Francorchamps in 1952. Although most manufacturers still use drum brakes, Girling has developed a disc brake for racing with BRM for use in the V-16. That car, however, is not here—a typical scenario at grands prix during this period. *Photo by Louis Klemantaski*

◀ For 1957 Maserati continued to develop the 250F as it entered its fourth season of Formula 1 competition. The latest chassis was stiffer and lighter and capable of accommodating Maserati's V-12 engine. The V-12 car seen here, parked rather inelegantly halfway down the transporter's ramp in a Monaco side street, is distinguished by the twin air scoops on the hood to feed two rows of carburetors. Although more powerful than the straight-six engine, the V-12 was heavier, and after practice for the Monaco GP, the team elected not to race it here. *Photo by Peter Coltrin*

▲ The Ferrari Dino 246s of Mike Hawthorn (4), Luigi Musso (2), and Wolfgang von Trips (6) sit in a field, ready for action in the 1958 French Grand Prix at Reims. As a temporary circuit, essentially a flat-out blast along a triangle of public roads, Reims offers little in the way of trackside garage facilities for the teams.

For this race Ferrari has modified the car's suspension in an effort to cure it of its tendency to understeer, but the nature of the circuit means that it is the Dino's powerful engine that carries the day. But this will be a race tinged with sadness and tragedy: Juan Manuel Fangio, the master, will retire from Formula 1 after hauling an uncompetitive Maserati 250F to fourth place; and Musso will die in hospital after crashing while negotiating a bend flat-out on the ninth lap. Hawthorn wins by 24 seconds from the Vanwall of Stirling Moss. *Photo by Peter Coltrin*

STIRLING MOSS

Some of us were professional. There were the Gordini and Ferrari teams, and HWM; and then you had guys on the side who weren't well-to-do, like Bruce Halford. He could afford to get an old Maserati, which he used to drive around in an ancient converted bus, doing moderate performances and picking up starting money here and there. But there were only three or four people like that, really.

STIRLING MOSS

We didn't have any worries about security. We'd take the horse box or the van with us to the hotel, and they'd usually have an enclosed area we could keep it in. I suppose some people occasionally got some tools stolen here or there, but I can't remember anyone losing a whole car. They were more likely to lose it in a road accident on the way than through theft.

FRANK WILLIAMS

The scene then was quite amateurish compared with today. There was far less development on the cars. The paddocks were very scruffy. Mostly they were just gravel.

We didn't even have an awning. Pretty much everything was out in the open, with our private road cars stuffed up against the side of the race cars. We'd have our debriefings in the road car or in the back of the garage—if we had one . . .

▲ Long before the days of electronic security gates, members of the public are free to wander and mingle with the competitors. In lieu of an awning, the Maserati 250Fs of Juan Manuel Fangio (2), Jean Behra (4), and Harry Schell (6) shelter from the June sunshine under the trees of the Rouen paddock during the 1957 French Grand Prix weekend. Owing to the cancellation of the Dutch and Belgian Grands Prix—thanks to differences of opinion over starting money—six weeks have elapsed since the previous World Championship race. *Photo by Louis Klemantaski*

FRANK WILLIAMS

The crowds were always huge. People loved entertainment and many of them loved cars, too. In the U.K. there were only one or two TV channels; they started at five in the afternoon and then at eleven o'clock it was, "Lights off, everybody go to bed." Racing cars went fast and made a lovely noise. Formula 1 drivers were starting to make the newspapers. The whole thing was burgeoning.

▶ The British public gets its first close-up view of the otherworldly Mercedes W196 "streamliner" that Karl Kling will drive in the 1954 British Grand Prix. It is only the car's second race outing, after taking a crushingly dominant debut win at Reims, but its slippery aerodynamic bodywork proves less suited to Silverstone. Both Kling and teammate Juan Manuel Fangio find it hard to place accurately, and they keep striking the oil barrels that are used as corner markers. In future Mercedes will reserve the streamliner for flat-out circuits such as Avus, Monza, and Reims.
Photo by T. C. March

JACK BRABHAM

There weren't the sponsors there are today. There was really only money from fuel companies. I raced with Esso at Cooper, and when we started our own team they gave us money towards that. We built smaller cars—Formula Junior, Formula 2—for sale so that we could get our own F1 car together.

◀ The Climax-engined Brabham BT7s of Dan Gurney (6) and Jack Brabham (5—Brabham is standing behind his car, in race overalls and white hat) are readied for the 1964 Monaco Grand Prix. The BT7 is only his eponymous marque's second F1 chassis and bears the hallmarks of engineer Ron Tauranac's approach. Note how the coil-over shock absorbers are mounted in a position that confers optimum geometry and strength, even though the airstream is slightly obstructed. At Lotus, Colin Chapman is mounting the moving parts of his suspension inside the bodywork, actuated by rocker arms, which gives an aerodynamic benefit but at some cost to driver "feel." *Photo by Colin Waldeck*

JACKIE STEWART

By the 1960s society had loosened off. The Beatles had arrived, the Rolling Stones had arrived. London was swinging. It was a relaxing of the sort of constipation that life had gone through in the aftermath of World War II. And that was recognizable in motorsport—it was glamorous, colorful, and exciting.

The long hair and sideburns, somehow that was all trendy, and the drivers became trendy. The sport was being televised regularly for the first time. It was getting a bit rock 'n' roll. Jim Clark and I were like Batman and Robin, even though he was very shy, almost introverted. People like Graham Hill and Innes Ireland—they knew how to have a good time.

▲ The Lotus team sets up in a quiet corner of Montjuich Park, Barcelona, for the second grand prix of the 1969 season. Formula 1 has come a long way in 20 years, but in many areas, particularly track facilities, it has not advanced a great deal. The Montjuich circuit is run on public roads in the city's famous park, and it has not been used for motor racing since the 1930s.

Designers are beginning to appreciate the role aerodynamics can play in generating cornering force as well as making cars quick in a straight line, but the high-mounted wings seen here on the Lotus 49s of Graham Hill (1) and Jochen Rindt (2) are primitive and vulnerable, as Hill and Rindt will find out when they both experience failures on race day. *Photo by Nigel Snowdon*

◀ Modern Formula 1 teams often complain about the cramped facilities at Monaco, but in 1957 the Maserati garage looks positively spacious—if not a hive of activity. The 250Fs of Carlos Menditéguy (36) and Giorgio Scarlatti (34) await attention.

Menditéguy, an Argentinian polo player of great repute, is a regular fixture at Argentine Grands Prix in the 1950s, but in 1957 he will make his way into a factory entry in Monaco, France, and Great Britain as well, having finished on the podium in the 1957 Argentine GP. He is famously gentler on his horses than he is on his cars. Scarlatti is less of a charger, and in this race the Italian privateer will be prevailed upon to hand his car over to Harry Schell after Schell's suspension breaks. *Photo by Louis Klemantaski*

◀ A mechanic fettles the engine of Louis Rosier's Lago-Talbot T26C (15) in the paddock at Silverstone for the 1950 British Grand Prix. Eight years earlier this had been farmland, until its rapid conversion in the early months of 1943 into an airfield, which, at the height of its activity, housed almost 60 Wellington bombers. After the base was closed in 1946, enterprising locals recognized the possibility of using the perimeter roads as a motor racing circuit.

Rosier will go on to finish fourth in the race, but Eugene Martin (17), making the first of only two championship Formula 1 starts, will retire with engine failure after eight laps. *Photo by Louis Klemantaski*

▶ Mechanics pause while working on the Lancia-Ferrari D50s at Monza in September 1955. It has been a tumultuous year in motor racing: Mercedes-Benz is withdrawing from the sport after the Le Mans disaster, and the death of Alberto Ascari prompted Lancia to throw in the towel and sell its cars to Ferrari.

The new circuit layout, which includes a pair of high banked curves and adds over two miles to its length, puts tires under unforeseen stresses and Giuseppe Farina crashes his D50 during practice. As a precaution Ferrari withdraws the cars from the race and Eugenio Castellotti (4), a pallbearer at Ascari's funeral, races in a Ferrari 555 instead, finishing third behind the Mercedes of Juan Manuel Fangio and Piero Taruffi. *Photo by Louis Klemantaski*

◄ British industrial magnate Tony Vandervell supervises work on the Vanwall Special to be driven by Peter Collins in the non-championship International Race Meeting at Goodwood, on September 25, 1954. An initial investor in BRM, Vandervell withdrew from that troubled organization and decided to build his own cars, beginning in 1950 with the "Thin Wall Special", a modified Ferrari named after one of his bearing company's most successful product lines. The Vanwall Special is a combination of a bespoke Cooper chassis with a range of engines based around Norton motorcycle and Rolls-Royce components.

Collins will finish second to Stirling Moss's Maserati 250F at Goodwood, but at the Spanish Grand Prix a month later he will crash during practice and damage the car beyond repair. Vandervell will subsequently acquire a 250F chassis from Maserati to strip down and analyse, and in 1958 the Vanwall team will win the inaugural Constructors' Championship with a car built entirely in-house. *Photo by Louis Klemantaski*

▲ BRM, a British national prestige project that has spent the decade promising much but delivering very little, arrives at Reims for the 1959 French Grand Prix on a high after winning its first F1 World Championship Grand Prix with Joakim Bonnier (due to drive car number 4 here) a month earlier. For its third season of racing the P25 is a much-improved machine, thanks in part to a detailed engineering revision in consultation with Lotus founder Colin Chapman, but 1959 is the year of the rear-engined revolution and the P25 will not win another grand prix, even with Stirling Moss at the wheel of a privateer entry. *Photo by Peter Coltrin*

▶ Giuseppe Farina leans meditatively against the concrete barrier at Monza in 1953. Nearly 47 years old, the 1950 champion has been overshadowed at Ferrari by Alberto Ascari, 12 years his junior. The Italian Grand Prix is the final World Championship round of the year and Ascari has already taken the title, having ignored team orders and passed Farina for the lead of the previous round at Bremgarten. The future of the team's involvement in Formula 1 is also in question; Enzo Ferrari has signaled his intention to withdraw from the sport at the end of the year. *Photo by Günther Molter*

▲ Juan Manuel Fangio (center) chats to Ferrari teammates Alfonso de Portago (left, sitting on car) and Eugenio Castellotti (right, holding gloves) before practice for the 1956 Italian Grand Prix at Monza. In the absence of Mercedes the year has been dominated by Ferrari and Maserati, and for this season finale Ferrari has entered seven cars.
Photo by Ami Guichard

STIRLING MOSS

It's true to say that the postwar years were rather austere, but we knew how to enjoy ourselves. Most of us were single, although Fangio had his partner. Not that we used the term "partner" back then; we just called her "Fangina." Jean Behra had a regular girl—Monique, I think her name was—and I remember once at Reims we utterly cleared out his hotel room before he arrived, took away everything that wasn't fixed to the floor. He took her upstairs and said, "Look at this lovely big suite I've got for us," and of course when she walked in there was nothing apart from a bidet . . .

STIRLING MOSS

There was tremendous camaraderie among the drivers. We were much closer than they are now. We'd go out on buying sprees together, or all eat out in the same place. We'd even negotiate bulk discounts together.

BRUCE McLAREN

Due to a filming appointment at Oulton Park on the Monday [after the 1962 British Grand Prix at Aintree], most of us congregated in the lounge of the Adelphi Hotel, and, with nothing to do, decided to visit Blackpool!

On the way back from a bleak afternoon spent scanning the bleak Riviera scene of bingo halls, Blackpool rock, and anatomical horrors in the wax works, the James Clark Lotus Elite was flagged down by a police car for allegedly touching 31 miles per hour in a restricted area. After a lecture on the evils of speed, the constable proudly finished berating his catch by saying, "You young fellows with fast sports cars don't appreciate the dangers of speed . . ."

▲ Ferrari's drivers prepare for the 1958 Monaco Grand Prix. Peter Collins sits on the left with his American wife, Louise, while Mike Hawthorn makes his way to the end of his book. In the middle, dressed for action although he is not entered for the grand prix, is regular Ferrari sports car racer Olivier Gendebien. Collins and Hawthorn have cause for optimism because the new car has won non-championship races at Syracuse (driven by Luigi Musso) and Silverstone (Collins), but it does not handle well enough around the streets of Monaco and they are pushed back to the third and fourth rows in qualifying. Hawthorn will briefly lead the race before Stirling Moss passes him, and then his fuel pump fails. Musso and Collins will follow Maurice Trintignant's Cooper across the finishing line in second and third. *Photo by Ami Guichard*

◀ Jochen Rindt (left) discusses business with his new Cooper teammate, the underrated American driver Richie Ginther, at Monaco in 1966. Cooper is no longer the dominant force it once was, and for this first year of the 3-liter formula has been forced to use the Maserati V-12—an engine that is almost a decade old in design, having originally been envisaged for use in the 250F. Against more modern motive force, neither the pace of Rindt nor the development capability of Ginther is able to provide much in the way of results this season. *Photo by Robert Daley*

◀ Bruce McLaren (left) and 1967 World Champion Denny Hulme examine the rear wing of one of their McLaren M7s at Silverstone in 1969. McLaren has followed Jack Brabham's lead in forming his own team and building his own cars, and after dominating the Can-Am sports car series the team has also come good in Formula 1. The engine is the key: after labouring with uncompetitive Serenissima and BRM engines, McLaren has secured a supply of Cosworth DFVs. Allied to the neat M7 chassis it forms a threatening package; and, fittingly, it was McLaren who took his marque's first World Championship Grand Prix win at Spa in 1968. *Photo by Nigel Snowdon*

CHAPTER 2

PRACTICE

"It was important to create a relationship with the engineers because you didn't have access to the kind of telemetry they have today. It all came from the seat of the pants—the driver's impressions."

—JOHN SURTEES

◀ Mercedes goes all out for success on home ground at the 1954 German Grand Prix with a four-car entry that stretches its resources to the limit. In "streamliner" form the W196 was unbeatable at Reims, less so at Silverstone. Here at the Nürburgring three open-wheeled variants have been readied for Juan Manuel Fangio (18), Karl Kling (19), and Hermann Lang (21).

Junior driver Hans Hermann (20) faces the tricky prospect of racing the less wieldy streamliner in only his third grand prix. Although the Mercedes team sets new standards in the level of its preparations, Hermann seldom feels the benefit: His was the only W196 to retire at Reims with mechanical problems, and it will do so again at this race after seven laps. *Photo by Yves Debraine*

Racing drivers place an implicit trust in the people who design, build, and maintain their cars. To be able to function at the top of their game, in the hostile environment of a racing cockpit, they must be able to direct all their attention to the process of driving. To be distracted by thoughts of what could go wrong is to be impaired—defeated long before the checkered flag.

In the first two decades of the Formula 1 World Championship, quixotic national prestige projects fought it out with ambitious manufacturer-backed teams; at the margins, under-resourced, backstreet *equipes* made do with what they could build or scavenge. Thrillingly, F1 proved that greatness could be achieved through sheer invention—that a team like Lotus,

from tiny beginnings in a North London lockup, could stand toe-to-toe with the likes of Ferrari.

Then, as now, success depended on who you worked with. The performance envelope of the cars was something that was explored and expanded on a race weekend through close communication between the driver and his mechanics rather than simulated back at the factory. Feeling the car, understanding the sensations it transmitted as it approached its limits, was a vital asset in a driver—as was a capacity to find ways of stretching those limits. It's hardly surprising that most drivers established working relationships with their mechanics that lasted for years, often taking key personnel with them when they moved between teams, or even building new teams around them.

◀ It's been four months since the first race of the season, in Argentina, as the Lancia team prepares for the 1955 Monaco Grand Prix. It's also the first time a grand prix has been held in the Principality since 1950.

To combat the all-conquering Mercedes, Lancia is fielding a team with strength in depth. Louis Chiron (32), is the only Monaco-born driver to have won his home grand prix, but at 55 he is nearing the end of a racing career that began when he married judiciously into money in the 1920s. Luigi Villoresi (28), 10 years Chiron's junior, is also a successful prewar driver and a personal friend of double World Champion Alberto Ascari (26). Although the fourth car pictured here bears the number 27, Eugenio Castellotti, Italy's latest racing darling, will drive car number 30. *Photo by Günther Molter*

STIRLING MOSS

A lot of the racing machinery in the early 1950s was still left over from before the war, until John Heath built the HWM. The problem was that you had to take standard bits and pieces and use them on the race car, and because they were then put under far more stress they tended to break. There were very few items you could buy that were purely for racing. The stub axles on the HWM were from a Standard Vanguard. Put on some tires that were very grippy for their day, and those components were undergoing far higher cornering forces than they had been designed to take. Sometimes it was more than they could stand.

STIRLING MOSS

To begin with, the fields weren't very big. We'd have maybe 15 entries. There was a real mixture of machinery. In 1952 I drove the ERA [G-type], which was dreadful. It was supposed to be very sophisticated and clever, so that it could make the most of the two-liter Bristol Formula 2 engine it was running. It was awful. The first time I raced it, the engine seized on the first lap. There was an awful lot of fuss about the project but it achieved very little, and I was disappointed to see other drivers doing better in much more basic cars. It taught me a valuable lesson: that even the cleverest concepts would not work without the money, manpower, and organization to develop them.

▲ A young Stirling Moss prepares for the rigors of road racing in the Ulster Trophy at Dundrod, Northern Ireland, in June 1952. The caravan seen in the background is typical of the low-tech team equipment of the time.

The combination of Moss and Juan Manuel Fangio ought to be a race-winner, but the BRM V-16's tenuous roadholding, fragile reliability, and abrupt power delivery does not endear it to its drivers. Moss will retire with an overheating engine after four laps but not before the gear knob comes off in his hand. Moss will later describe the BRM organization as "just not up to the job." *Photo by Louis Klemantaski*

▶ The field assembles for the Belgian Grand Prix at Spa-Francorchamps in June 1954, five months after the first grand prix of the year. It is an event that straddles two eras: New engine rules have attracted fresh interest to a championship that has had to be run to Formula 2 rules during 1952 and 1953, but the much-anticipated entries from Lancia and Mercedes-Benz have yet to arrive.

The professionalism of Mercedes will redefine what is expected of a top-level team. Ferrari hedges its bets: the 625 is an adaptation of the 1953 title winner, its engine enlarged to 2.5 liters; the 553 is purpose-built for the new rules. Froilán González (6) will take the lead at the start in his 553, but its engine will seize on the first lap. Maurice Trintignant (8) will finish second in the venerable 625, behind the Maserati 250F of Juan Manuel Fangio. *Photo by Louis Klemantaski*

STIRLING MOSS

Mercedes operated at a much higher level. They had a fantastic chief engineer, Rudi Uhlenhaut, and we were allowed a great deal of freedom. I could have whatever gear ratios I liked, not just in the rear axle but in the gearbox itself. I could choose any steering ratio I wanted. We had complete control over the car. It was still not an easy car to drive, particularly in the wet, because of the swing-axle suspension. But very little went wrong, and the team were brilliantly organized. I remember coming into the pits with my hands and face covered in brake dust, because the drum brakes were mounted inboard, and there was a fellow waiting for me with a bowl of warm water and a towel.

Every practice lap you did was timed and counted as a qualifying lap, so you could compare how well you were exploiting the potential of the car just by looking at the times of other people in similar cars. If someone went out and was a couple of seconds faster, you'd know they were really pushing, and that you'd have to try harder to catch them; if they were slower you'd be quite happy. You judged your own speed by that of your competitors. The limits of performance weren't so clearly and scientifically defined as they are now.

▶ Mercedes racing manager Alfred Neubauer confers with Stirling Moss during practice for the 1955 Monaco Grand Prix. A meticulous organizer, Neubauer leaves nothing to chance. In the prewar era he pioneered the art of pit-car signals, and during the second coming of Mercedes in 1954–1955 his team's consistently high level of operational efficiency is a model for others to aspire to. *Photo by Alan R. Smith*

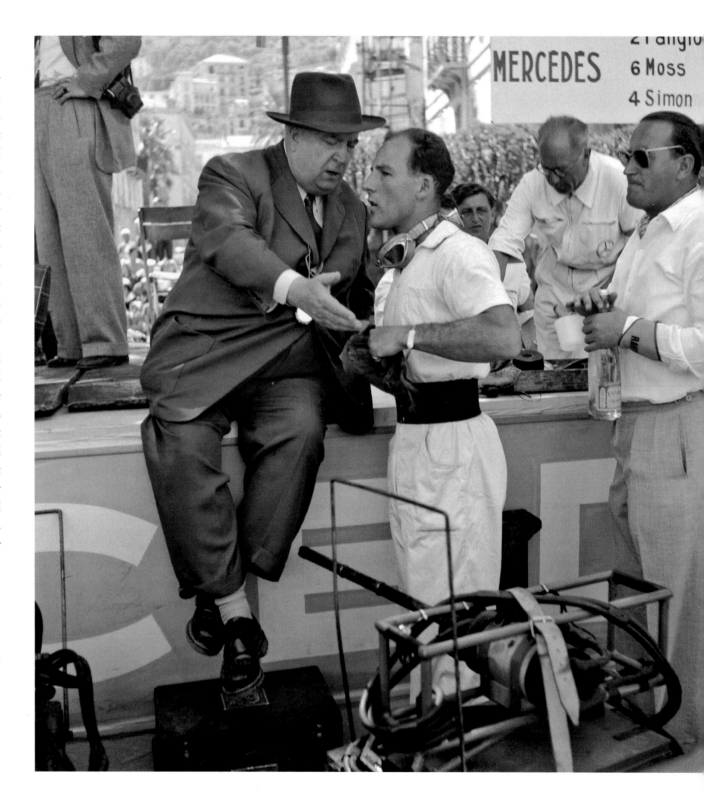

▲ Although at most races in this era every practice lap can count toward a position on the grid, at Monaco in 1955 it is announced that only Thursday's laps will inform the starting order. For Alberto Ascari, therefore, there is little time to waste if he is to get in amongst the dominant Mercedes. Juan Manuel Fangio proves tantalizingly out of reach, but Ascari manages to demote Stirling Moss to a starting position of third. It is to be one of Ascari's last acts as a racing driver. He will crash out of the race—landing in the harbor—while disputing the lead with Moss, and the following Thursday he will suffer a fatal accident while testing a sports car at Monza. *Photo by Ami Guichard*

◄ Maserati has made a big push for 1955, entering as a factory rather than merely selling to privateers. This is its answer to the Mercedes "streamliner" that has been so dominant on the high-speed circuits: a 250F with wind-cheating bodywork, to be driven at the Italian Grand Prix by Jean Behra.

Beneath the skin, the car has an ominous past. Although entered as chassis 2518, it is actually chassis 2512; the car in which Onofre Marimón was killed at the Nürburgring in 1954, and which Sergio Mantovini crashed at Turin. Mantovani survived the accident but lost a leg, ending his career. The car suffers persistent cooling problems and its engine blows up just as Behra is about to cross the finish line in fourth place. It will make two more appearances in non-championship grands prix before being destroyed in a factory fire. *Photo by Yves Debraine*

▲ Practice also provides an opportunity to evaluate new machinery against the competition; here, at the 1957 Monaco Grand Prix, Juan Manuel Fangio tests the V-12–engined Maserati 250F. He will revert to the straight-six for the race. *Photo by Louis Klemantaski*

FRANK WILLIAMS

The sort of people who worked on the cars were either mechanics or specialist tradesmen—sheetmetal workers and so on. Mostly it was just the mechanics who came to races, although we always took a fabricator with us. The tires were quite simple to operate; you got about three sets for the weekend. It wasn't the industry it is now.

There were five people on our team, plus Piers Courage's wife, who did the timekeeping. I bought and sold racing cars at the time, so I did have other people working for me, but the racing team was just five people. That was quite enough. The engines came down from Cosworth and we did the transmissions ourselves. They were much simpler cars to look after. We bought our first from Brabham. It was a year old. It wasn't a very expensive car to run; Ron Tauranac had engineered it very well.

The Ford DFV changed the face of Formula 1. It enabled people like me to turn up and have a go at it. That engine had a completely new level of engineering. It blew away everything that went before it. It was cheap and it was clever.

▶ Ferrari chief mechanic Luigi Parenti directs work on the Lancia-Ferrari 801s of Maurice Trintignant (16) and Mike Hawthorn (14) during practice for the 1957 French Grand Prix at Rouen. Note the stopwatch-wielding timekeepers at bottom right. *Photo by Louis Klemantaski*

▲ It is the 1958 Belgian Grand Prix, and 31-year-old Maria Teresa de Filippis is about to make history by becoming the first woman to drive in a Formula 1 World Championship race. Believed to be one of Luigi Musso's mistresses, the Italian's qualifying lap in the privately entered Maserati 250F is 30 seconds off Mike Hawthorn's pole position time; for a non-professional, on the challenging and dangerous 8.7-mile Spa-Francorchamps circuit, this is probably to be expected. *Photo by Edward Eves*

▲ A technician checks the tire pressures on the Ferrari D246 of Peter Collins during practice for the 1958 British Grand Prix at Silverstone. During this era teams are beginning to understand the importance of pressure in maximizing the tire's contact patch. Having tried the Dunlop tires, Ferrari will revert to Engleberts for the race, although Collins' teammate Mike Hawthorn believes the Dunlops to be slightly faster. *Photo by Edward Eves*

▲ Rob Walker's mechanics work on the Cooper-Climax T51 that Stirling
Moss will drive at the 1959 Monaco Grand Prix. The Cooper's rear-engined
layout confers traction and agility, and the new 2.5-liter Coventry Climax
engine is competitive and fairly reliable. Moss will qualify on pole position but
retire from the lead with gearbox problems after 81 of the 100 laps, allowing
Jack Brabham through to take his first World Championship win, also in a T51.
Photo by Peter Coltrin

◀ Phil Hill (left) and a thoughtful-looking Dan Gurney (right) chat with Ferrari engineer Carlo Chiti at the 1959 Portuguese Grand Prix. As a constructor, Ferrari is slow to embrace the rear-engine format, and will plug on with the front-engined Dino 246 until the end of the 1960 season. Its V-8 engine has a power advantage, but despite adopting disc brakes and changing from Englebert to Dunlop tires, the car is no match for the agility of the rear-engined Coopers this season. Gurney will just edge out Hill in qualifying to start from sixth on the grid. *Photo by Peter Coltrin*

▲ The look on Lance Reventlow's face says it all as he tries to have a quiet moment during a hectic 1960 Monaco Grand Prix weekend. A product of a complicated family tree—his biological father is a Danish nobleman and his mother, who was briefly married to Hollywood actor Cary Grant, is the heiress to the Woolworth fortune—Reventlow has commissioned the Scarab, America's first Formula 1 car. The heavy front-engined beast is practically a dinosaur even as it makes its debut this weekend; Stirling Moss has tried it, and although he lapped quicker than Reventlow and Scarab's second driver, Chuck Daigh (right), his time would not have been enough to put the car on the grid. *Photos by Robert Daley and Yves Debraine*

BRUCE McLAREN

The first practice session [at the Nürburgring in 1962] was on Friday morning, and all the teams were hard at work sorting their respective cars out—checking how much lower the bump stops should be set and how long the springs were to be to avoid bottoming out on the bumpy sections.

I started my second practice run a few seconds after Graham Hill had taken off in the BRM. The Cooper V-8 sounded crisp and it was handling nicely. I was just starting to get with it, swooping into the Fuchsrohre, when a huge cloud of dust in front spelled trouble with a capital "T" and I jammed the brakes on, stopping a little farther up the hill to see Graham and the BRM virtually out of sight behind the trees.

Graham had come whistling down through the curves to find a large 16mm movie camera [which had fallen off Carel Godin de Beaufort's Porsche] lying in the middle of the track. I suppose he must have been doing around 140 miles per hour, and he straddled the camera rather than run a wheel over it. Unfortunately, racing car ground clearances aren't designed to cope with movie cameras and it ripped the bottom out of the oil tank.

If I'd been any closer to Graham I probably would have had less warning and ended up in the ditch with the BRM. As it was, my teammate Tony Maggs came down the hill flat out just at the moment when the flag marshal had "taken five" from waving the oil flag to phone control. Tony arrived at speed to discover the contents of the BRM oil tank. The result was that two cars were written off, two drivers were miraculously unharmed, and the oil had put paid to any serious practice for the rest of the day.

◀ The much underrated Innes Ireland finds a humorous way of acknowledging the uncompetitiveness of his BRM-engined British Racing Partnership car at Rouen in 1964. BRP, originally founded by Stirling Moss's father and manager, ran customer chassis until 1963 and then built its own. The best Ireland can wring out of the car is 11th on the grid. *Photo by Yves Debraine*

▲ It's early in the Italian Grand Prix weekend at Monza in 1963 as Graham Hill speaks to BRM's Tony Rudd. Following team owner Alfred Owen's win-or-else ultimatum and the elevation of Tony Rudd to oversee operations, the team found competitive form in 1962 and Hill won the World Championship. Hill's defense of his title has proved somewhat fraught in the face of renewed opposition from Jim Clark, whose Lotus has been much more reliable. Many of those concerns have had to be shelved during practice, though, after several cars suffered suspension damage on the bumpy concrete banking. Late on Friday afternoon the organizers announced that the race, which was planned to use the combined road course and banking, will now run solely on the road course. It means hours of hard work for the mechanics, who will now have to alter gearbox and transmission ratios; disruption for the tire suppliers, who must now provide tires of different sizes; and tension for the drivers, who have been informed that because of the reduced circuit length, only 20 of the 30 entries will be allowed to start. *Photo by Peter Coltrin*

▲ Colin Chapman (left) and Jim Clark (wearing helmet) discuss the order of work before the first practice session of the 1964 Monaco Grand Prix, with Clark's mechanic Cedric Selzer (between Clark and Chapman) in close attendance. *Photo by Robert Daley*

JACK BRABHAM

I had a very good relationship with my mechanics, maybe because I'd come from a mechanical background. I worked very closely with the same group of people for many years. We had a lot of guys from Australia and New Zealand in the team.

Our biggest drama was working with an engine company [Repco] 12,000 miles away from where we were actually racing. That created a lot of problems for us; the airfreight side of it was always a bind. I often think back and wonder how the hell we actually won a world championship with all the problems we had; twice we had engines lost between Melbourne and London.

One time the plane carrying our engines had technical trouble in Cairo. They put the passengers on another plane, but all the cargo, including our engines, went back to Melbourne. Another time, I insisted on being there when they actually loaded the engine onto the plane. When I got to the other end they said there was no engine. I rang British Airways every day for three weeks, asking them where it was. They said they didn't have it. Then I got a call saying, "We've had an engine here for three weeks. When are you going to pick it up?"

JOHN SURTEES

There wasn't a great difference in approach between the factory teams and the private teams, but the small British teams were more focused than the Ferraris and Hondas of this world. Trying to get those manufacturers to focus was a problem because they were both their own worst enemies.

The operational agility of the British teams gave them a big advantage in the chassis design, and having the engines by Coventry Climax, then the Cosworth that came later, that made things much easier for them. Everyone else had to catch up. When I went to Ferrari, they didn't have a chief engineer any more—Carlo Chiti had walked out. Probably good riddance to him.

Ferrari's program was a bit of a mish-mash. We had to do endurance racing, which was pleasurable, but I didn't like the fact that it took all the effort away from Formula 1. Nothing happened to the F1 car until after Le Mans. It was a very disjointed team. I tried to change it and I had a bit of success, introduced a bit of different thinking, but that alienated some people and perhaps it led to me leaving in the end.

It was a similar thing with Honda. They used racing as a design team exercise and were so far removed from the scene that we had to put a team together over here. They were superb engineers but we suffered in some ways from overengineering and a lack of practicality. Their first 3-liter V-12 used lots of concepts like the center power takeoff, which was similar to the prewar Alfa Romeo, because they'd been told to run a roller-bearing crankshaft and you have problems taking the power from the end with those. We ended up carrying about 200 pounds more weight than the opposition.

When I started the project with Lola and Yeoman Credit, I brought in a couple of mechanics who I'd met when I first tested the Aston Martin. Later on I brought them in on the Honda, too. There was a core of people who came through; when I started my own team I recruited a lot of people I'd worked with before. It was important to create a relationship with the engineers because you didn't have access to the kind of telemetry they have today. It all came from the seat of the pants—the driver's impressions.

◀ John Surtees contemplates his Ferrari 312 at Spa-Francorchamps in 1966. Despite winning the 1964 title with the team, his fractious relationship with team manager Eugenio Dragoni is plumbing new depths. He also believes the new V-12 is too heavy and not powerful enough. Nevertheless, he is three seconds faster than his closest rival in practice, and will go on to win the rain-soaked race in dominating fashion. It is not enough to keep him at Ferrari, however, and after another argument with Dragoni at Le Mans he walks out, never to return to the marque. *Photo by Ami Guichard*

JACKIE STEWART

Choosing who you were going to drive for was very important. The old saying is that to finish first, first you must finish. I got an offer to drive for Lotus, but I wanted to drive a car that I had real confidence in. Ken Tyrrell produced a car that was very robust, and which I could drive. In those days, if you went off because of a mechanical failure, the impacts were so heavy that no car could sustain it. So you couldn't afford a mechanical failure. You'd drive for somebody who you had confidence in. The level of preparation and the quality of the mechanics at Tyrrell was superb.

The whole thing, from the machine tooling to the fabrication of the car, was probably done by six people—four of whom were the mechanics who operated it at the track. I had Roger Hill, Max Rutherford, Roy Topp, and Roly Law looking after me as mechanics. I always said they were better at what they did than I was at what I did.

I recognized at a very early age that it was important to work with the right people. If you fly with the crows, you'll be shot at; you're judged by who you mix with, who you work with, and who you do business with. That's why I've always been careful to work with good quality people, and why I can remember all their names 40 years later.

▼ Graham Hill has become accustomed to wet races in 1968—this, at the Nürburgring, is the fifth consecutive grand prix to be affected by bad weather. Therefore he sits quietly under an umbrella, waiting to see if practice will actually take place. *Photo by Nigel Snowdon*

▶ Jackie Stewart tightens his own wheel nuts during practice for the Tasman series race at Warwick Farm in February 1967. He will win the race from pole position in his Reg Parnell–run BRM P261, beating Jim Clark's Lotus. *Photo by Nigel Snowdon*

"You just had to keep both eyes on the man holding the flag."

–STIRLING MOSS

◄ The remarkable Stirling Moss occupies pole position at the 1961 Monaco Grand Prix in his privately entered Lotus 18, having left the factory teams in his wake during practice. Next to him, waiting for the start, are Richie Ginther in the Ferrari 156 and Jim Clark in the works Lotus 21. The BRM and Ferrari of Graham Hill and Phil Hill watch from row two. All that remains is for the ever-colorful Louis Chiron to flag the field away… *Photo by Ami Guichard*

For as long as there have been grands prix, many of the participants have been fighting the urge to vomit during the final minutes before the most crucial point: the start. Hearts race as the adrenalin surges; it is a response every bit as primordial as a wild animal's instinct to fight or flight.

In the 1950s and 1960s, long before electronic systems stripped the starting process down to its reflexive essence—see light, hit button—a grand prix driver faced an enormous number of variables and potential hazards. The journey ahead had not been painstakingly mapped by a computer simulation; in fact, if they could get by without visiting the pits, they would. They were on their own.

And yet they were not alone. They would line up on the grid three abreast with their fellow competitors, many of whom they knew well and socialized with. The circuits were often public roads rather than permanent facilities, with corners bounded not by gravel run-off areas but by someone's driveway or garden wall. Spectators lined the route, close enough to touch, and photographers would stand close enough to set foot on the road. The first lap would be a true adventure as the drivers elbowed their way through.

To all these hazards, add the unknown: spontaneous clutch failures, overheating engines, gearboxes that would break or fail to engage, driveshafts that would shear under duress. Each of these potential factors awaited the drivers as they licked their lips and eyed the starter's flag apprehensively, waiting for the merest twitch, all played out to the soundtrack of screaming engines.

Balancing the feet, perfectly judging the interplay of clutch and throttle, deftly managing the nervous equilibrium of cold tires on warm asphalt? That would be the easy part.

◀ Luigi Fagioli's Alfa Romeo 158 is rolled out to take its place on the grid for the first World Championship Grand Prix at Silverstone in 1950. Neither the car nor its driver are strangers to action; the car shown here was commissioned and built in the prewar era and concealed to prevent it being melted down for munitions, while 52-year-old Fagioli had been Rudolf Caracciola's teammate and rival at Mercedes in the 1930s. Although not one to obey team orders gladly, Fagioli will playfully duke it out with Giuseppe Farina for the lead before following his team leader across the line. *Photo by Alan R. Smith*

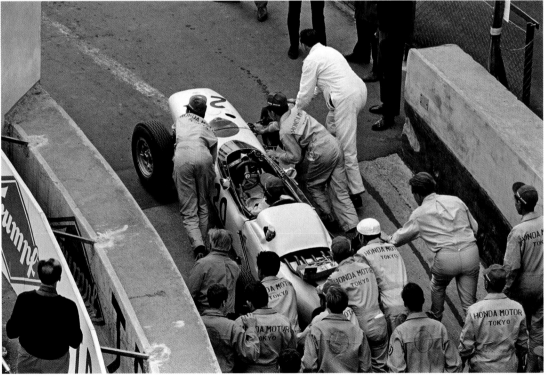

◀ There are scenes of great excitement at the 1964 German Grand Prix as Honda's new Formula 1 machine is pushed out in public at last. The public is eager to see what the manufacturer—already a world champion in motorcycle racing—can do in F1. The car has already been much-modified after running on the circuit before official practice, during which its suspension bottomed out so frequently on the Nürburgring's innumerable bumps and dips that its exhausts broke. American driver Ronnie Bucknum, a rookie at this level, will suffer persistent engine problems during practice and barely make the grid. *Autosport*'s Gregor Grant will later write, "The car sounded very crisp, but I am inclined to think that several of the Japanese horses escaped from the stable." *Photo by Günther Molter*

▶ Over a month after the end of the 1957 Formula 1 World Championship, many of the drivers are back in action for the Moroccan Grand Prix at Casablanca. Jean Behra's Maserati 250F is pushed to the start, while Behra himself (right) walks alongside Rob Walker, whose team is fielding Jack Brabham in a Cooper. Several other drivers have been struck down by a mystery illness: Stirling Moss will not take the start, while Juan Manuel Fangio, Harry Schell, Peter Collins, and Mike Hawthorn struggle through the race. Behra will take a convincing victory ahead of the Vanwall of Stuart Lewis-Evans; it is a kind of last hurrah for Maserati, which has announced its withdrawal from F1 after doing much to ensure the health of the sport from the change of formula in 1954 onward. In the early months of 1958 the company will go into receivership. *Photo by Edward Eves*

▶ Graham Hill drives his new BRM P261 through the back streets of Monaco to the track while a mechanic pilots Richie Ginther's car; the lack of space for a paddock means that teams have to rent local garages in which to prepare their cars for the race. *Photo by Robert Daley*

▲ Peter Collins and Stirling Moss are among the brightest hopes for the home crowd at the British Grand Prix in 1956, although the press remains curiously optimistic about the prospects of Mike Hawthorn and Tony Brooks in the underachieving BRMs. Moss, now with Maserati works support, will put his 250F on pole position and lead for 53 laps before falling behind Juan Manuel Fangio and then succumbing to a fuel leak seven laps from the end of the three-hour race; Collins' engine seizes on lap 64 but he takes over teammate Alfonso de Portago's car and finishes second. *Photo by Alan R. Smith*

▲ Mike Hawthorn, with his distinctive bow tie, has a hand on soon-to-retire Juan Manuel Fangio's shoulder during the drivers' briefing for the 1958 French Grand Prix. Peter Collins and Harry Schell have also made their way to the front. Stirling Moss is just behind Collins, alongside Roy Salvadori and Tony Brooks. In the white helmet, some way behind Fangio, is American driver Troy Ruttman, who has earned points in the Formula 1 World Championship through participating in the Indy 500 (becoming the youngest ever winner of that race in 1952, at the age of 22). Yet since it is highly unusual for F1 drivers to race at Indy, this is the first time he has come face to face with his "championship rivals" on a road course. He will finish 10th in a Scuderia Centro Sud Maserati 250F and never race an F1 car again; but his record for being the youngest winner of an F1 World Championship event will stand for another 45 years. *Photo by Edward Eves*

STIRLING MOSS

There seemed to be a better rapport between the drivers and the FIA in those days. I remember we went to them and said that the guy who qualified on pole position should be able to choose whether they started on the left or the right of the front row, and they agreed. The drivers seemed to have more say, or at least they felt that they had a say.

▲ The apprehension on the drivers' faces (including, from left to right, Jochen Rindt, Bob Bondurant, Jo Siffert, John Surtees, Phil Hill, Graham Hill, Lorenzo Bandini, Dan Gurney, Mike Spence, and Jo Bonnier) is palpable during the pre-race briefing at Spa-Francorchamps in 1966. A scarily quick circuit even in fine weather, it is treacherous in the wet and rain is on the way. Only seven of them will still be running at the end (See chapter 8). *Photo by Robert Daley*

JACKIE STEWART

I did have a routine that I'd go through before the start of the race. I liked to satisfy myself that everything was in order. Before the race, the last thing I'd do before pulling on my gloves was to take my watch off and give it to Ken [Tyrrell] to look after, knowing that the first thing he'd do when I returned was to give it back to me.

◀ Peter Collins (2) and Eugenio Castellotti (3) prepare for the start of the 1956 German Grand Prix at the wheel of their Lancia-Ferrari D50s, but team leader Juan Manuel Fangio allows himself a moment of quiet contemplation before climbing aboard. Stirling Moss, on the far side of the grid, is the fastest of their rivals in his Maserati 250F.
Photo by Louis Klemantaski

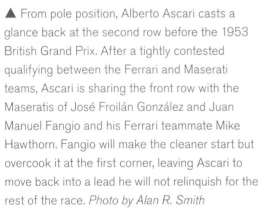

▲ From pole position, Alberto Ascari casts a glance back at the second row before the 1953 British Grand Prix. After a tightly contested qualifying between the Ferrari and Maserati teams, Ascari is sharing the front row with the Maseratis of José Froilán González and Juan Manuel Fangio and his Ferrari teammate Mike Hawthorn. Fangio will make the cleaner start but overcook it at the first corner, leaving Ascari to move back into a lead he will not relinquish for the rest of the race. *Photo by Alan R. Smith*

▲ Mike Hawthorn dispels the tension on the start line of the non-championship 1953 *Daily Express* International Trophy at Silverstone by showing the officials a magazine centerfold featuring a young lady *au naturel.* To his right is the Cooper-Bristol of British Hill Climb Champion Ken Wharton (36), who despite being only an irregular privateer entrant in F1 at World Championship level, has outqualified Hawthorn by a second. Hawthorn, though, will win both this heat and the final. *Photo by Alan R. Smith*

▲ Harry Schell awaits the start of the 1956 *Daily Express* International Trophy at Silverstone in his Vanwall VW1. These are the days before sophisticated electronic timing separates drivers by the split second, and Schell's 1m42s in qualifying puts him on equal pole with Stirling Moss in the other Vanwall, a VW2. These are early days for the marque, though, and Schell will be forced out with a sheared fuel pipe after 19 laps. *Photo by Louis Klemantaski*

▲ Eugenio Castellotti mulls over his race strategy before the start of the 1956 British Grand Prix at Silverstone. His Ferrari teammates Peter Collins and Juan Manuel Fangio are on the front row of the grid, while his eighth-fastest time places him on the third row. In his determination to get to the front he will go off-course at Club and buckle the chassis, then face the final indignity of having to hand his car over to Alfonso de Portago, who has given his Ferrari to Peter Collins after Collins' Ferrari lost oil pressure (see chapter 8). *Photo by Louis Klemantaski*

▲ Stirling Moss adjusts his goggles on the Goodwood grid, ready for the 21-lap Richmond Trophy on Easter Monday, 1955. He will rocket away from Roy Salvadori at the start, but his Maserati 250F's engine will sputter to a halt when its fuel-injection pump fails. *Photo by Alan R. Smith*

▲ Three weeks after losing his friend and teammate Peter Collins at the Nürburgring, Mike Hawthorn looks pensive as he adjusts his Ferrari's mirrors on the grid at Porto. He will finish second to Stirling Moss's Vanwall, enabling his rival to make up ground in the title race with just two points-scoring opportunities left in the season. *Photo by Edward Eves*

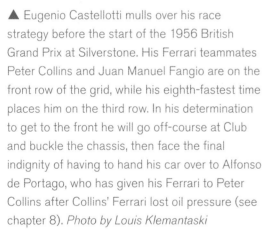

BRUCE McLAREN

An incident on the grid 10 minutes before the start [of the 1962 British GP] raised a laugh. For ease of entry the Porsche steering wheel was detachable, rather like a knock-on wire wheel. Dan Gurney's steering wheel and its big three-eared wing nut were sitting on the nose of the Porsche, and for devilment Jimmy Clark "borrowed" the wheel and nut and vanished into the grid crowd.

He threw me the wheel nut and passed the wheel to someone else, and before long no one—least of all Dan—knew where the Porsche tiller was. Poor Dan was in quite a state, but when the five-minute board went up we took pity on him and returned his steering gear.

Dan Gurney falls victim to Jim Clark's prank on the grid at the 1962 British Grand Prix; the steering wheel for his Porsche has been returned—but where is the missing retaining nut? *Photos by Robert Daley*

JACK BRABHAM

My mood before a Grand Prix was mainly excitement and looking forward to the race. Once I was in the car I couldn't wait to get going. For the start itself it was important to have a clear head, even though it was enormously exciting, because getting the car away from the line involved a lot of skill and judgment.

▲ "Black Jack" Brabham relaxes in the final moments before the start of the 1960 Dutch Grand Prix. The field is rather denuded because the organizers announced that while they would allow 20 cars to start the race, only the fastest 15 in qualifying would be paid starting money. Therefore Lance Reventlow has withdrawn his Scarabs (the fastest of which was three seconds slower than Stirling Moss's pole lap) and Roy Salvadori has packed up his Aston Martin. This will be Brabham's first grand prix win of the year. *Photo by Robert Daley*

STIRLING MOSS

Some drivers got so nervous before a race that they almost threw up. I'm glad I never felt like that. I was apprehensive beforehand, but once the flag fell there were no nerves or anything like that—only if you scared yourself by going too quickly and losing control. There was certainly a lot to think about as you formed up on the grid, with all the other competitors around you. It was very easy to get distracted, to look down at your instruments or something. You just had to keep both eyes on the man holding the flag.

◀ The pressure of racing at home: Wolfgang von Trips keeps his eye on the starter at the 1961 German Grand Prix. From fifth on the grid he will bring his Ferrari 156 home in second position, chasing the winning Lotus of Stirling Moss in vain as rain envelops the circuit in the final laps. *Photo by Robert Daley*

◀ The Vanwalls of Stirling Moss (3) and Harry Schell (4) share pole position at the 1956 *Daily Express* International Trophy at Silverstone. Schell has already crept forward, eyes intent on the starter's flag, while Juan Manuel Fangio (1) and Mike Hawthorn (9) remain in formation. Moss, in contrast to his teammate, looks totally relaxed. *Photo by Alan R. Smith*

▶ Ferrari has already won the constructors' championship, but at the penultimate race of the 1961 season the drivers' championship is an open contest between two Ferrari drivers: Phil Hill and Wolfgang von Trips. The crowd at Monza is thrilled to see its favorite team lock out the front two rows; Von Trips (4) is on pole, ahead of Ricardo Rodriguez (8), Richie Ginther (6), and Phil Hill (2).

But the joy is soon to be overtaken by tragedy; Hill, Ginther, and Rodriguez pass the slow-starting von Trips, who spends the opening lap dueling with the Lotus of Jim Clark, who started seventh. As they approach the Parabolica—only part of the way around a lap that also includes the recently renovated banked oval—the Lotus and Ferrari touch. Von Trips is thrown from his car as it spears off the circuit and into a spectator enclosure, killing him and 14 others. *Photo by Robert Daley*

◀ Possibly the most daunting view from any Formula 1 grid: the run down to the legendary Eau Rouge corner at Spa-Francorchamps. By the 1990s, in the era of wings and slick tires and active suspension, drivers will describe this perilous dip as "easy-flat." Here, on June 17, 1962, Jim Clark (center of frame, third from right, without gearbox cowling) is about to make history.

Graham Hill in the BRM V-8 is almost out of view in pole position, alongside fellow front-row starters Bruce McLaren (Cooper-Climax) and Trevor Taylor (Lotus-Climax). All year, poor mechanical reliability has prevented Clark from fully exploiting the potential of his beautifully minimalistic Lotus 25, the first F1 car with a monocoque chassis. Having missed most of practice while waiting for a new Climax engine to arrive from England, Clark is starting 12th, with the wily Jack Brabham just behind him and the orange Porsche of Dutch aristocrat Carel Godin de Beaufort to his right.

Spa is a network of public roads bordered by hedges, houses, and telegraph poles; not so lethal as the Nürburgring, its near neighbor in the Eifel Mountains, but still dangerous. Clark sets any reservations aside and makes an explosive start to run fifth by the end of the first lap, passing Hill when the BRM's V-8 starts to cut out intermittently, then on past McLaren and the Ferrari of Willy Mairesse. Taylor waves him through to the lead, then suffers a mechanical failure while battling with Mairesse and they both crash out—Taylor's car knocks down a telegraph pole—leaving Clark with an unassailable lead over Hill. It is the first victory for a car with a monocoque chassis. *Photo by Günther Molter*

◀ José Froilán González (5) and Reg Parnell (6) demonstrate the art of the perfect getaway in the five-lap Woodcote Cup Formula Libre race at Goodwood on September 27, 1952. Teammate Ken Wharton's BRM V-16 has failed to fire up (a depressingly regular occurrence for the marque) and has been pushed away from the grid, leaving a gap for Giuseppe Farina's Thin Wall Special (2). *Autosport*'s report vividly captures the moment seen here: "As the starter raised his flag, Farina took his eyes momentarily from the flag to check his instruments. That split second was fatal. The BRMs were already on the move before the Italian banged in his clutch, the car absolutely standing still with smoking rear tyres." *Photo by Alan R. Smith*

▶ Jack Brabham (8), Graham Hill (1), Dan Gurney (9), and polesitter Jim Clark (4) smoke their tires away from the start of the 1963 British Grand Prix at Silverstone. Clark's getaway, in front of his home crowd, is a poor one, and he will drop to fifth place on the opening lap as Brabham takes command from Gurney, Hill, and the fast-starting Bruce McLaren. *Photo by Colin Waldeck*

◀ Stirling Moss spins his Vanwall's wheels as he takes command of the 1957 Glover Trophy race at Goodwood. He and teammate Tony Brooks are destined to lose a commanding one-two position with troublesome throttle linkages. Unreliability also plagues the BRMs of Ron Flockhart and Roy Salvadori. This grievous wound to national pride is reported solemnly in the next week's edition of *Autosport:* "It may confidently be predicted that some pretty serious action will be taken at Acton and Bourne to remedy the troubles so depressingly revealed in a comparatively short race of 77 miles." *Photo by Louis Klemantaski*

JACKIE STEWART

I learned how to remove emotion, because emotion is one of the most dangerous things in life. Whether it's fear before the start, or you find yourself thinking, "I'm leading and there's only a few laps to go; I've got things in the bag." That's poor mind management, and you have to learn to remove that. I won most of my races in the first five laps because everybody else was still winding down from the overly hyper condition they'd got themselves into before the start.

▲ The front row lights up its tires as the 1965 British Grand Prix gets underway. Richie Ginther (11) is the odd man out in this photograph: He is the only driver in it never to win the drivers' championship. Jim Clark (furthest from camera) is on pole position with his Lotus 33-Climax, just two races away from winning his second drivers' title in the final season of the 1.5-liter era; beside him is the BRM P261 of 1962 champion Graham Hill, who will move to Lotus and win the title again in 1968; nearest the camera is Hill's teammate, Jackie Stewart, the champion in 1969, 1971, and 1973. In fifth place, carrying the number one on his Ferrari by dint of being the incumbent champion, is John Surtees.

Ginther uses the power of Honda's technically ambitious and high-revving V-12 to make an excellent start and briefly leads the race before Clark passes him; although destined not to win here, Ginther takes Honda's first F1 victory at the final race of the year, in Mexico. Clark will hold on to win despite being troubled by a misfire in the closing laps. *Photo by Colin Waldeck*

▲ Polesitter Jackie Stewart (7) makes the better getaway from the front row to lead the 1969 Monaco Grand Prix in his Matra-Ford MS80. Chris Amon (11) gets more wheelspin in his Ferrari 312 but still holds on to second place. Both are destined to retire, though: Stewart and teammate Jean-Pierre Beltoise suffer driveshaft failures and Amon's differential breaks, enabling Graham Hill to win for Lotus. *Photo by Yves Debraine*

▲ Chaotic scenes at the start of the 1960 French Grand Prix at Reims as starter Toto Roche has dropped his flag immediately after the 30-second board has been displayed. The Cooper of Jack Brabham (16) and the Ferrari of Phil Hill (2) sprint away into the lead, but fellow front-row starter Graham Hill's clutch has been dragging and his engine stalls as he tries to engage first gear. Wolfgang von Trips (4) dodges the melee to move to third place from seventh on the grid. In the midfield, Bruce Halford and Maurice Trintignant tangle, and the latter drives straight into the back of Hill's immobile BRM. Brabham, Phil Hill, and von Trips spend the early part of the race in a superb 180-mile-per-hour slipstreaming battle until the Ferraris fade with mechanical trouble. *Photo by Günther Molter*

▲ Grandstands more accustomed to the roar of sports cars at the annual 24-hour race reverberate to the scream of Formula 1 engines as the 1967 French Grand Prix gets underway on an attenuated version of the Le Mans circuit. In the center of the frame, Graham Hill (7) makes a clean start from pole position in the remarkable Lotus 49. Jack Brabham is alongside in his Repco-engined BT24, with Dan Gurney's Eagle on his left. Brabham will snatch the lead from Hill but Jim Clark, starting here on the row behind Hill, will pass them both. Brabham will get his lead back when the Lotuses encounter gearbox trouble.
Photo by Louis Klemantaski

◀ Jean Behra (4) snatches the lead in his Maserati 250F rounding the first turn of the French Grand Prix at Rouen-les-Essarts on July 7, 1957. Ferrari's Luigi Musso (10) leads the pursuit from polesitter Juan Manuel Fangio (2), Peter Collins (12), and Mike Hawthorn (14).

Roy Salvadori (20) has quit BRM for Vanwall, lining up with Stuart Lewis-Evans (18). Both Vanwall's regular drivers are unavailable for work; Stirling Moss is suffering sinus problems after a waterskiing accident, and Tony Brooks is recovering from injuries sustained when his Aston Martin flipped at Le Mans. *Photo by Louis Klemantaski*

◀ The field bunches together at the Gasworks Hairpin immediately after the start of the 1960 Monaco Grand Prix. Jo Bonnier's BRM is out of sight from fifth on the grid, having pre-empted the starter's flag, while polesitter Stirling Moss has been swallowed up by the pack and is just visible here behind the Cooper of Jack Brabham (8). Tony Brooks (18) takes the outside line in the BRP Cooper. Moss's team boss Rob Walker has decided to change his Cooper for a Lotus 18 and Moss is a revelation in the privateer car, chasing down Bonnier for the lead and then only briefly relinquishing it to Brabham before claiming the win. *Photo by Günther Molter*

▲ In the absence of a single administrative body—the FIA has yet to take control of operational procedures during World Championship Grands Prix—starting procedures can be fraught. Here, at Spa-Francorchamps in 1958, the field has managed to get away cleanly despite being held on the grid for five minutes after the organizers first displayed the two-minute board. Stirling Moss leads his Vanwall teammate Tony Brooks up the hill, chased by local hero Olivier Gendebien in his bright yellow Ecurie Belge–entered Ferrari 246. Moss will retire after missing a gearchange later on this lap, while Brooks goes on to take Vanwall's second-ever GP victory at an average speed of 129.93 miles per hour—making this the fastest road race ever held in Europe. *Photo by Yves Debraine*

CHAPTER 4

RACECRAFT

"When you're competing at a top level you need to know, fairly intimately, those you can trust, those you need to stay clear of, and those who you can bully or take liberties with."

–JOHN SURTEES

◀ Spectators enjoy the view as Stirling Moss (6), driving the short-wheelbase version of the Mercedes-Benz W196, sizes up the Vanwall of Mike Hawthorn (18) at the 1955 Monaco Grand Prix. Moss is already running second at this point; having been held up by Eugenio Castellotti in the Ferrari he is some way behind teammate Juan Manuel Fangio. Unusually, both Mercedes will succumb to mechanical failure. *Photo by Alan R. Smith*

For all that Formula 1 is a machine-dependent sport, there is one quality that cannot be simulated or otherwise subsumed by technology: racecraft, the art of defeating your opponent effectively through guile.

Until the 1960s, most grands prix ran to three hours. Besides being an immense physical effort, racing was mentally draining. And there was so much to think about: preserving the car to the finish while lapping at the fastest possible speed; trying to understand where one was in relation to the nearest rivals, given the primitive communications of the time; and how to pass the drivers ahead without getting entangled with them.

An intimate knowledge of your rivals' disparate skill sets and mentalities could be a crucial advantage: knowing which weak spots to probe, where to hang back and where to attack; and, of course, whether the overtaken driver would accept defeat or immediately fight back. The dangers, always attendant when driving these cars at speed, multiplied when running in close proximity with others. At this point there was, perhaps, a transition: where knowledge of another person's mindset has to become an implicit trust that they will not do something reckless to foil the overtaking maneuver—if, indeed, they've seen it coming in the first place.

Even the best drivers suffered from "brain fade." But there were many others who, even on a good day, required an approach in which aggression was tempered with caution. This being a close-knit sport, though, their foibles were usually well known . . .

GRAHAM HILL

I have a little mental card index for every driver. No driver responds in exactly the same way, so I have this little mental index which I look up whenever I come upon another driver so that I know what to expect from him. If you know all this, obviously you're not going to put yourself in a position which might be very embarrassing. This might sound terribly self-righteous, and I don't intend it to be, but very often a lot of near misses can be anticipated, and this comes through experience with the people you're driving against.

▶ Alberto Ascari (2) cracks a sly grin as one of the Alfa Romeos—most likely Juan Manuel Fangio (38)—creeps alongside his Ferrari 375. The World Championship lead is delicately poised between Fangio and Ascari at the penultimate grand prix of 1951, at Monza. The season has been a fascinating contest between the prewar Alfa Romeos, their 1.5-liter engines hopped up with twin superchargers and volatile fuel additives, and the 4.5-liter V-12 Ferrari 375s. Fangio starts from pole position in his Alfa, but Ascari is immediately on his tail in the Ferrari from third on the grid. The battle will rage until Fangio's engine fails on the 39th lap. *Photo by Louis Klemantaski*

STIRLING MOSS

It was important to know who you were racing against. Racing drivers are a very small band of people. Even if you took all the races I did, there were only a couple of hundred other drivers. You knew everybody, unless it was someone coming along for the first time.

I knew the styles and the personalities, and it was vital. Willy Mairesse was an absolute madman, so obviously I'd give him a wide berth. You had to watch out because he really didn't understand what the hell he was doing. Other people you'd get to know, analyze their strengths and weaknesses, their presence of mind. You could work out who you could outbrake, who you'd have to sell a dummy to.

You never want another driver ahead of you. You catch them and pass them. That's what it's all about. I think it was Jackie Stewart who has talked about winning at the slowest speed possible; to my mind that's not racing.

◀ Alberto Ascari (34) leads Ferrari teammate José Froilán González (32) in the early laps of the 1954 Italian Grand Prix, pursued by Juan Manuel Fangio (16) in the Mercedes W196 "streamliner" and Stirling Moss (28). Before the advent of modern safety features, the trees and undergrowth at Monza are unsettlingly close to the track. *Photo by Yves Debraine*

▶ The 1953 French Grand Prix at Reims thunders toward a riveting conclusion as Mike Hawthorn (16) and Juan Manuel Fangio (18)— who almost appear to be in conversation—charge down the final straight side by side. It has been an epic slipstreaming battle. Hawthorn will bring his Ferrari across the line just a second ahead of Fangio's Maserati after nearly three hours of racing in the energy-sapping July heat. *Photo by Louis Klemantaski*

▲ In the days before sophisticated communications it's often hard for spectators to understand the ebb and flow of a race—and never more so than when drivers swap cars during the course of it. Here, at Monaco in 1956, Eugenio Castellotti (20) is now driving the car started by Juan Manuel Fangio. Car 26, which was started by Peter Collins, may at this point have Fangio at the wheel. Castellotti's clutch failed on the 14th lap, and he inherited Fangio's car after Fangio hit the wall at the chicane. Ferrari then called Collins in from second place to give his car to Fangio. This complicated act of teamwork isn't enough to wrest the win from Stirling Moss, but it delivers second place to Collins and Fangio, who by the end is reeling Moss in at a rate of two seconds a lap. *Photo by Louis Klemantaski*

▶ Overtaking is tricky at Monaco so a good qualifying position and a clean start are vital for success. Here Mike Hawthorn (38) has left himself with a lot of work to do after the start of the 1958 Monaco Grand Prix. He started sixth, but Ferrari teammate Luigi Musso (34) has passed him for position from tenth on the grid. Harry Schell (8) started his BRM 12th. *Photo by Yves Debraine*

STIRLING MOSS

There are very few real *racers* in the world, as opposed to mere racing drivers. They're the people who have a ruddy good go. I don't mean to say that the others aren't trying, because they are; but they don't have the mental ability to push to the same extent, to really take it to a higher level. In my day it would be Juan Manuel Fangio, who to my mind was the best driver there has ever been; and Jean Behra was a real racer, too. Others, when you passed them, you didn't really consider where they were. But with Behra you had to watch your mirrors, because he'd be trying to take you back.

◄ Jean Behra's BRM (14) dives as he stands on the brakes at Reims in 1958. Behind, the Vanwall of Stuart Lewis-Evans (12) looks rather less dramatic. Note the tire marks from where other drivers have skidded off; braking is an imprecise science in this era as manufacturers move from drums to discs. Behra will dispute second place with Juan Manuel Fangio and Stirling Moss (while Mike Hawthorn leads) before his fuel pump breaks nine laps from the checkered flag; Lewis-Evans is called in to hand his car over to Tony Brooks, whose gearbox has failed. *Photo by Peter Coltrin*

◄ Later in the same race, Behra (14) is now challenging Stirling Moss (8) for second position. The famous La Garenne restaurant is a distinctive background feature of Thillois corner, the last overtaking opportunity before the main straight. Behra, as Stirling Moss attests, is not a driver who can be overtaken and forgotten about: He will always look for a way back past. *Photo by Peter Coltrin*

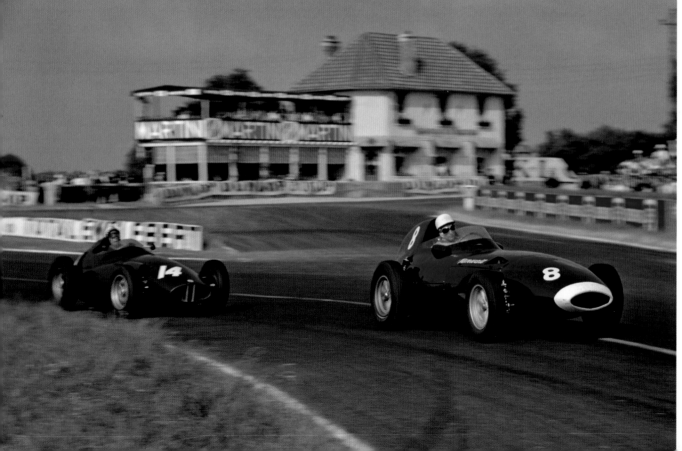

▶ Streetlamps, cobbles, and tramlines add to the challenge of the makeshift Porto street circuit, with the extra complication of rain on the morning of the 1958 Portuguese Grand Prix. Here the track is drying as eventual winner Stirling Moss (2) harries the Ferrari of Mike Hawthorn, who after the deaths of teammates Luigi Musso and Peter Collins in cars bearing the number 2 has requested a last-minute change of race number from 22 to 24; he will finish the race a lap down in fifth place. *Photo by Edward Eves*

▶ The 1958 Formula 1 World Championship will be decided at the final race of the year, on public roads in the barren countryside outside Casablanca in Morocco. Stirling Moss has a chance of taking the title if he wins and sets fastest lap and Mike Hawthorn finishes no higher than third. Moss duly races into the lead while Hawthorn (6), here shadowed by the BRM of Jo Bonnier (18), sits back and allows his Ferrari teammate Phil Hill to head the pursuit. Moss's teammate Tony Brooks also comes into play, passing Hawthorn and challenging Hill until his Vanwall's engine lets go. When Hill allows Hawthorn through to second, it is left to the third Vanwall of Stuart Lewis-Evans to peg him back. Tragically, Lewis-Evans' engine seizes and sends his car off the road, where he is covered in burning fuel from the ruptured petrol tank. Despite the best efforts of the medical profession back in the U.K. he succumbs to his injuries days later. Bonnier finishes fourth, behind Hill, and goes on to take BRM's maiden GP win in 1959. *Photo by Edward Eves*

▲ Driving an obsolete car, Stirling Moss drives the race of his life at Monaco in 1961. With the side panels of the privately entered Lotus 18 removed to keep his legs cool, Moss takes the lead on the 14th lap and then has to approach each of the 86 remaining ones like a qualifying lap to keep the Ferraris of Phil Hill and Richie Ginther behind. Moss's Climax 1.5-liter engine has a deficit of around 35bhp compared with the Ferraris. Behind him, the Ferrari pit is furiously signaling its drivers to go faster, and occasionally directing them to swap places for a fresh assault on the blue Lotus. *Photo by Günther Molter*

◄ Power tells at Reims, and although the front-engined Ferraris are outmoded in 1959, Tony Brooks (24) has enough grunt at his disposal to lead the French Grand Prix from pole position, chased by Jack Brabham (8) in the diminutive rear-engined Cooper that has been the surprise of the season. Phil Hill (26), here ahead of Stirling Moss (2) and Masten Gregory (10), will use the Ferrari power to bump Brabham down to third by the end of the race. It is 90 degrees Fahrenheit in the shade, and although the organizers have wisely cancelled the 12-hour sports car race that usually supports the GP, the track surface is still breaking up; Gregory will retire on the eighth lap after being hit in the face by a stone and suffering the effects of the heat. *Photo by Yves Debraine*

STIRLING MOSS

My best race was certainly Monaco 1961. If I'd done 100 laps at the same speed as I'd done pole position, I'd only have been 40 seconds quicker. I had two Ferraris within three seconds of me for 100 laps, so I was under a lot of pressure. That was a really interesting race.

I could see them behind me every time I went through the hairpin. Richie Ginther would be ahead, then Phil Hill. I didn't realize that they were saying to each other, "Okay, now you have a try." I didn't take the lead until about lap 12, and then I thought, "Right, I've got to do a perfect lap every lap from here." Of course, you can't do that, but trying to do it helped me keep my concentration up. I could gauge the progress of the Ferraris from where they were in relation to the street furniture as I looked up from the hairpin. Sometimes I'd gain a few feet, sometimes I'd lose a few feet. It was nerve-wracking and very exciting.

JOHN SURTEES

I had a 25-second lead in Portugal, my second GP, and I made a mistake while lapping Stirling, who'd had a pit stop. I was having a few problems in that some oil or fuel had got onto my boots and the pedals were a bit slippery. The main straight was long and it had tramlines down it, then you turned off it to take the back section past all the sardine factories. That was a really fast part of the circuit where you could make your time up, but there was a 90-degree right-hander.

I'd come up behind Stirling before, and I didn't want to sit behind him because I had a rhythm going. I just wanted to get going. I slipstreamed up behind him and then pulled out to overtake, but I did it too slightly. I should have done it more sharply because as I crossed the tramlines the wheels caught a little, which slowed down the steering as I came to turn in. I understeered and clipped the curb, which knocked the radiator hose off. That was pure inexperience.

▲ Grand prix newcomer John Surtees (18) chases Stirling Moss (12) around the streets of Porto in the 1960 Portuguese GP. The pair had disputed the lead earlier in the race, but now Moss is about to be lapped after a long pitstop to have faulty spark plugs changed. Moss is not keen to be lapped, and Surtees, who has already broken the lap record, does not want to be distracted by a fight. After a brief tussle Moss pits again and then emerges to find himself circulating in company with Surtees once more. The tramlines visible on the right will play a role in what happens next…
Photo by Robert Daley

BRUCE McLAREN

By the time things had settled down [in the 1967 Monaco GP], I had managed to work out where I was. [Jackie] Stewart and [Denny] Hulme were dicing for the lead, [Lorenzo] Bandini and Surtees for third place, and I was right behind Surtees.

The Honda and Ferrari could out-accelerate me once they got onto the seafront, but I could catch them around the Casino and down the hill. They were holding me up a little bit, but there was no way I could get past. Then the Honda started spewing something that looked like water, so I dropped back for a bit to let it get that over. It stopped spraying, but it wasn't long before a lot of blue smoke started to appear and it wasn't accelerating as well as it had been. [Jim] Clark was starting to catch me, so I just had to get by the Honda somehow.

I knew this was going to be a scene because the only possible place to pass was going into one of the hairpins, and on my high bottom gear I couldn't turn sharply and accelerate at the same time without the engine hesitating. The only thing I could do was slip the clutch and get the rear wheels spinning the moment I turned.

Fortunately, it worked, and I got by Surtees to have a go at Bandini . . .

▲ The BRM engine in Bruce McLaren's M4B (16) is almost a liter smaller than those in the cars in front of him, making his performance in the 1967 Monaco Grand Prix all the more extraordinary. Here he is sizing up the Honda of John Surtees (7), who is battling for third with Ferrari's Lorenzo Bandini. *Photo by Nigel Snowdon*

JOHN SURTEES

It was one of the major difficulties I had. Before my first car race, I hadn't actually *seen* a car race before. Everybody was a stranger. When you're competing at a top level you need to know, fairly intimately, those you can trust, those you need to stay clear of, and those who you can bully or take liberties with.

▲ Stirling Moss (16), Juan Manuel Fangio (18), Piero Taruffi (14), and Karl Kling (20) pound around the southern banking at Monza in their Mercedes-Benz W196s. This, the 1955 Italian Grand Prix, is a farewell tour for Mercedes, which has decided to withdraw from racing after the Le Mans disaster. Moss leads from Fangio, Taruffi, and Kling on the first lap, then Fangio moves to the front. The long straights of Monza's road course usually make for pitched slipstreaming battles, but this combination of the road course with the oval has thrown chassis science and tire construction into the mix: Ferrari has been forced to park its more competitive ex-Lancia D50s because their tires could not handle the cornering force on the banking.
Photo by Yves Debraine

▲ At these speeds, on these roads, you need to be aware of the skills and foibles of those around you. Ferrari teammates Juan Manuel Fangio (10), Peter Collins (14), and Eugenio Castellotti (12) charge down the main straight from Thillios corner at the 1956 French Grand Prix. Reims, based on public roads cutting through largely flat agricultural land, is a classic slipstreaming circuit where one car can use the hole in the air made by the one ahead to build up speed and pass. In this era it is still considered ungentlemanly to block such maneuvers. Collins and Castellotti will finish 1–2 after being ordered to maintain position by the team in the final laps, Fangio having slipped back after pitting to repair a fuel leak. *Photo by Yves Debraine*

▲ The Lancia-Ferrari D50s of Luigi Musso (28), Eugenio Castellotti (24), and Juan Manuel Fangio (22) thunder along the start-finish straight at Monza in the climactic 1956 Italian Grand Prix. A slipstreaming circuit such as this requires tactical discipline as well as bravery: Musso and Castellotti will expend their tires in their battle for the lead and have to pit for replacements. Castellotti will crash out when one of his new tires fails at high speed, but take over car 22 when Fangio brings it into the pits with a broken steering arm on lap 19 of 50. Fangio expects to take the wheel of car 28 from second-placed Musso, but the Italian refuses to hand over. At this point fourth Ferrari driver Peter Collins comes in and gives his car to Fangio; karma then deals Musso a blow when his steering arm breaks, allowing Fangio through to finish second behind Stirling Moss and seal the World Championship. *Photo by Günther Molter*

▲ A dramatic final act is about to unfold under the usual blazing skies of Reims in the 1961 French Grand Prix, tempting spectators and fellow racers—including Stirling Moss (top left, with shirt unbuttoned), Willy Mairesse (in front of the woman on crutches), and Tony Brooks (fifth from right), who have retired from the race—out of the shade, dangerously close to the action. Jim Clark has dropped back from the leading battle in his Lotus after a stone smashed his goggles; the fight for the win is now between the Ferrari of GP debutant Giancarlo Baghetti (50) and the Porsches of Joakim Bonnier (10) and Dan Gurney. All three drivers will take turns in the lead during the tense slipstreaming battle, although Bonnier's engine will expire with three laps to go. 300 yards from the finishing line, Baghetti will dive out of Gurney's slipstream and cross the line a fraction of a second ahead. *Photo by Robert Daley*

"Being introduced to a car was like being introduced to a new person. You had to communicate with it, learn about it, get it to talk to you."

–JOHN SURTEES

◄ Jochen Rindt cajoles his Cooper T77 into a slide at the 1965 British Grand Prix. His calculated aggression is never in doubt, but this race will end in retirement for him 17 laps from home when his Climax engine lets go. By the end of the decade he will be guided by his manager, Bernie Ecclestone, away from the waning Cooper marque and become the subject of a fierce contractual tug-of-love between Brabham and Lotus. *Photo by Colin Waldeck*

Experts talk about "feel" as if it is something that can be quantified or qualified, plotted on a graph and held up for comparison between drivers. The truth is that the drivers themselves often cannot articulate how they do what they do. They simply get on and do it.

In this era the cross-ply tires gave up their grip far earlier but usually more progressively than the radials that were to come. A good driver could detect all the impulses that came through the chassis and steering—the sensation of weight transfer under braking and acceleration, the compliance of the suspension, the hint of sidewall squidge as the tires bit into the asphalt and made the car turn.

An even better driver could interpret this stream of data and make the car dance—string together the near-mythical ten-tenths lap in which every movement is as close to the car's absolute limit as possible without stepping over the edge. Later, experts would define this process of instinctive delicacy as "managing the dynamic weight of the car."

In most cars this demanded precision, economy, and fluidity of input into the controls; others could readily be bullied into it. Some cars really had to be taken by the scruff. Understanding this, too, was what separated the great drivers from the merely good. Whether they chose to adapt the car to suit their style, or vice versa, was up to them.

◀ With almost clinical precision, Juan Manuel Fangio runs the edge of a wheel over the grass verge on the Reims circuit's curving section between Gueux and La Garenne during the 1951 French Grand Prix. His fastest lap of this 4.86-mile circuit is an average of 118.95 miles per hour—and yet he drives every lap of this 3-hour, 22-minute race with the same immaculate precision, despite a chronic misfire that will eventually persuade him to take over teammate Luigi Fagioli's Alfa Romeo 159. *Photo by Louis Klemantaski*

◀ The weight of the streamlined bodywork and the curiously antiquated swing-axle suspension conspire to make the Mercedes-Benz W196 a handful, but Juan Manuel Fangio's face gives away nothing of this as he negotiates the fast right-hander at the end of the start-finish straight during the 1954 French Grand Prix at Reims. Fangio will take a commanding victory at this race, the much-anticipated comeback of Mercedes to top-level competition; but the car is less effective at Silverstone and is replaced by an open-wheeled variant (seen below, also driven by the master, at the Swiss GP at Bremgarten) for twistier circuits. Despite the W196's tail-happy nature, Louis Klemantaski still gets as close to the apex as he can . . .
Photos by Louis Klemantaski

▶ Fangio holds his Lancia-Ferrari in a beautifully controlled drift, just inches from the curb, around Mirabeau at Monaco in 1956. Shooting from a hotel balcony, Louis Klemantaski perfectly captures Fangio's extraordinary precision at a moment when the slightest error could bring the car's delicate wheel into sharp contact with the street furniture.
Photo by Louis Klemantaski

◀ In 1958 the diminutive but agile mid-engined cars produced by British manufacturers thoroughly out-handled their front-engined rivals. The tipping point comes in 1959, when Climax produces a larger engine; Stirling Moss, seen here at Casino Square, leads the Monaco Grand Prix after qualifying on pole. *Photo by Ami Guichard*

STIRLING MOSS

It didn't pay to be too rough with some cars. Jack Brabham was quite rough, but he could do that with the Cooper, because it was an easy car to be rough with. If he'd treated a Lotus like that he would have had a lot more problems. The Cooper was very suited to his style. I made my style suit the car I was in.

▲ Jack Brabham has won the World Championship two years in succession but here, at the 1961 Dutch Grand Prix at Zandvoort, the reality must be sinking in that Ferrari has better adapted to the new 1.5-liter engine formula. Brabham is a more brutal driver with his machinery than some of his rivals, and that can be seen clearly here in his determined facial expression and purposeful grip on the steering wheel as he negotiates Tarzan corner. *Photo by Günther Molter*

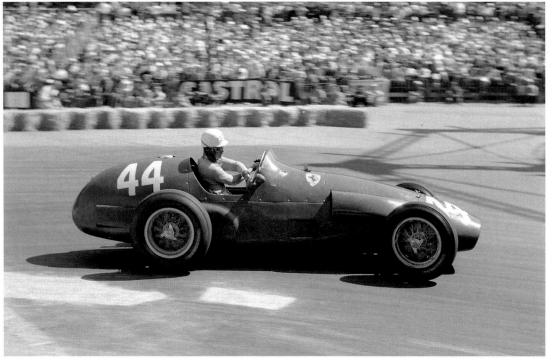

◀ Juan Manuel Fangio (top) calmly steers his Mercedes W196 around the Gazomètre hairpin on the throttle during the 1955 Monaco Grand Prix; compare and contrast with eventual winner Maurice Trintignant (left), who is all crossed up in his understeering Ferrari. *Photos by Alan R. Smith*

▶ Relaxed, smooth, and controlled in spite of running in close proximity to Juan Manuel Fangio, his illustrious teammate, Stirling Moss looks unruffled by the pressure of racing in his home grand prix for Mercedes in 1955. He will lead the four W196s—including Fangio's—across the finishing line. *Photo by Louis Klemantaski*

Some people liked to throw the car around. But I'd seen Farina drive. He looked so relaxed. I sort of modeled my style on his. I liked to lean back, in the straight-arm position, because that way you had more control than if you were close by. Smoothness was everything.

▶ To beat the all-conquering Alfa Romeos in 1950 and 1951 you had to be utterly committed; José Froilán González is demonstrating just that as he flings his Ferrari sideways at 140 miles per hour, tires almost peeling off the rims, through Silverstone's Abbey corner during the 1951 British Grand Prix. On the apex an oil drum awaits to catch the unwary. González will be rewarded by victory—the first time Alfa has been beaten since the World Championship began. *Photo by Louis Klemantaski*

STIRLING MOSS

The Maserati 250F was a beautiful car to drive. You could persuade the tail to step out very easily. The Vanwall was a more difficult car to drive, more abrupt and unpredictable in its responses, and its gearbox was unpleasant to use.

◀ A fast exit from Tabac is essential for achieving a good speed down Monaco's harbor-front start-finish straight, but the paved surface lacks grip, especially in the wet. Equipped with his well-balanced Maserati 250F, Juan Manuel Fangio makes even this incredibly long power drift look almost easy. *Photo by Peter Coltrin*

▶ Jean Behra's commitment is unshakeable at the 1957 French Grand Prix at Rouen, although his Maserati 250F is slowed by a broken exhaust pipe and a down-on-power engine. The 250F wins surprisingly few World Championship races during its career, largely owing to patchy reliability, but drivers all praise its ability to be steered on the throttle. *Photo by Louis Klemantaski*

◀ Mike Hawthorn is really having to push to keep up with Ferrari teammate Peter Collins at the 1958 British Grand Prix at Silverstone; the public are expecting a Hawthorn vs. Moss duel for the win, but Collins will cross the line first despite being ordered to slow down to preserve his engine after Hawthorn is forced to pit for an oil top-up. *Photo by Edward Eves*

◀ Following his promotion from the Formula 2 ranks as part of Ferrari's push for victory in the 1958 Italian Grand Prix, the understated American driver Phil Hill lets his driving do the talking as he throws his Dino 246 sideways into Monza's Parabolica corner. Hill will charge back up to third place at the finish after dropping to 10th during an enforced pit stop to replace a badly worn tire. *Photo by Yves Debraine*

▶ Jack Brabham power slides his Cooper around the Hunze Ruc corner at Zandvoort in 1959. The Dutch track's location on the North Sea coast means that drivers face a relatively unusual hazard for a grand prix circuit: Sand from the nearby dunes blows on to the surface, making it unpredictably slippery. *Photo by Günther Molter*

◀ Chuck Daigh's Scarab lifts a wheel as he muscles the overweight, underpowered car up the hill from Eau Rouge in the 1960 Belgian Grand Prix. No amount of finesse is going to help: Daigh started last after qualifying 28.5 seconds slower than Jack Brabham's pole position time, and the ill-sorted beast is destined to retire when its engine breaks on lap 16. *Photo by Louis Klemantaski*

◀ Dan Gurney has been spending the 1964 Monaco Grand Prix weekend playing catch-up after missing Thursday's practice because of his Indianapolis commitments. During the 1.5-liter era the cars have become slimmer and lower, and fully independent suspension permits a wider track; even so, while the wheels stay roughly perpendicular to the ground, the angle of the car's body demonstrates the cornering forces. Gurney will take the lead from Jim Clark's Lotus, to rapturous applause from the American sailors watching from the deck of the aircraft carrier USS *Enterprise* moored in the harbor, but he is forced to retire when his gearbox fails and an oil pipe sprays hot lubricant all over his legs, burning him badly. *Photo by Colin Waldeck*

◄ Packing 51 corners, many of which are hairpins, into its five-mile length, Clermont-Ferrand is a very different proposition from Reims, the circuit it has (temporarily) displaced as home of the French Grand Prix in 1965. Nevertheless Jim Clark looks totally relaxed as he leads the race—even though he is doing so in the spare Lotus after his race car's engine failed during practice. *Photo by Yves Debraine*

◄ Denny Hulme shows why he is nicknamed "The Bear" as he hustles the fat-tired McLaren M7A around Monaco in 1968. The car's handling has been woeful and prone to understeer throughout the weekend—not a useful trait around these tight streets—and both Hulme and McLaren have spent most of practice in the pits, tinkering with the suspension settings to persuade it to oversteer. Hulme's car has a special shortened nose to aid cooling. Attrition enables him to run as high as third before he has to pit for a driveshaft change, but since only four other cars are running he is able to get going again and complete just enough laps to be classified in fifth place. *Photo by Nigel Snowdon*

BRUCE McLAREN

After the initial disappointment [of retiring from the 1963 British GP] wore off, I stood and watched Clark, Brabham, Gurney, [Graham] Hill, and Surtees fighting for the lead. They reminded me of a Brockbank cartoon.

Jimmy came through with his mouth open, and occasionally his tongue between his teeth. The tires were holding a tenuous grip on the road with the body and chassis leaning and pulling at the suspension, like a lizard trying to avoid being pried off a rock. Then Dan arrived, really throwing the Brabham into the corner, understeering and flicking the car hard until he had it almost sideways, then sliding through with the rear wheels spinning and the inside front wheel just on the ground.

Jim Clark (top), "driving with superb artistry, completely devoid of fireworks, but tremendously fast," according to *Autosport's* Gregor Grant, leads the 1963 British Grand Prix at Silverstone in his Lotus 25. The chasing pack—Brabham's Dan Gurney (bottom), World Champion Graham Hill (opposite top) in the BRM, and John Surtees (opposite bottom) in the Ferrari 156—vividly demonstrate how each car responds at the limit. *Photos by Colin Waldeck (top and opposite) and Nigel Snowdon (bottom)*

◀ A special kind of finesse—and courage—is required to maximize a car's potential in wet conditions. Two weeks after winning the season-opening Argentine Grand Prix for Mercedes-Benz in blazing sunshine, Juan Manuel Fangio is back in action—this time in driving rain—for this two-heat Formula Libre race in Buenos Aires. Formula Libre events draw mixed grids of cars; some new, some obsolete. Mercedes is trialing a new 3-liter engine, derived from the 300SLR sports car, in the W196. Despite the World Champion's legendary touch, he will be beaten by teammate Stirling Moss in the second heat—but on combined time will emerge the overall winner. *Photo by Günther Molter*

◀ Only his slightly open mouth betrays the mental effort involved as Jim Clark steers his Lotus to victory in the wet at Zandvoort in 1965. He will win by a commanding margin. Jackie Stewart—himself no slouch in the rain—is eight seconds down the road and cannot get any closer. *Photo by Yves Debraine*

JOHN SURTEES

Someone who understands a car and is sympathetic to it will relish that relationship with it. That's one of the satisfactions of being a racing rider or a driver—sensing the reactions of the car and directing it so that you maximize its potential. Being introduced to a car was like being introduced to a new person. You had to communicate with it, learn about it, get it to talk to you.

Adapting styles comes around when you're having to deal with problems that arise, which in those days happened a lot. The car would communicate with you; it would send you a message. And that coming together between you and the car would be the thing that provided the ultimate performance. You didn't need a car that was easy to drive. Often a car that was easy to drive wasn't very quick. Sometimes a car that was a bit tip-toey when it was getting to its limits was the quicker car. It was your relationship with it that allowed you to extend it beyond 100 percent when required.

▲ The Ferrari 312 of John Surtees leads the denuded field in the 1966 Belgian Grand Prix. A sudden storm struck midway through the first lap, triggering multiple accidents that eliminated eight of the 15 starters—including Jackie Stewart, who suffered chemical burns (see Chapter 8). On the drying track Surtees is peerless, and having caught and passed the early race leader Jochen Rindt, he will win by 42 seconds. *Photo by Ami Guichard*

"There's a very fine line between bravery and stupidity. They're almost the same thing. Sometimes they *are* the same thing."

—STIRLING MOSS

◀ After trying the V-12–engined Maserati 250F in practice for the 1957 French Grand Prix at Rouen, Juan Manuel Fangio opts to race the six-cylinder car and sets an average speed of slightly over 100 miles per hour on his way to victory. *Photo by Louis Klemantaski*

Thanks to narrow, lightweight bodies and skinny tires, the Formula 1 cars of the 1950s and 1960s were not much slower in a straight line than their modern equivalents. The shift to 1.5-liter unsupercharged engines for 1961 drew criticism from competitors, but in truth it merely accelerated a process that was already underway: the transition from cumbersome spaceframe chassis with back-of-an-envelope aerodynamics to elegantly minimalist darts had begun in earnest when Jack Brabham won the 1959 Monaco Grand Prix in a Cooper T51.

Without the brutal power of large multi-cylinder engines and toxic fuel additives, F1 had to embrace cleverer chassis constructions and aerodynamic efficiency. Over a decade after starting out as a playground for leftover prewar machinery, the World Championship properly became the pinnacle of automotive technology. The speeds began to creep up again and the drivers learned to like it.

The 1.5-liter era briefly pegged back acceleration, but the widespread adoption of disc brakes brought a dramatic reduction in braking distances, and improved tire compounds and better-balanced chassis yielded faster cornering speeds. In short, it provided more ways for the drivers to test their mettle.

The term "adrenaline junkie" was yet to be coined, but it aptly describes the character of these racers: willing to hurtle at dazzling speeds around dangerous circuits in machines that offered little in the way of crash protection.

For them, risk was something they accepted—even embraced. Danger was an attraction in itself.

139

◀ Harry Schell charges through the tight confines of the Glade at Crystal Palace in the non-championship 1955 London Trophy. Hazards are rife in this section of the track: To his left there is a tree-lined bank, while to his right, beyond a smattering of Victorian lamp posts, the ground falls steeply away to a small lake. His Vanwall VW2 is good enough to win his heat, but in the final he fluffs his start and is beaten into second place by Mike Hawthorn, who is driving a Maserati 250F on loan from Stirling Moss. The famous glass house that gave the park its name is long gone, having burned down in 1936. Safety fears, the development of a new sports center and athletics stadium, and complaints from local residents about noise will eventually put an end to racing in this busy South London suburb. In a final act of cultural vandalism the local council will block the circuit and reduce the width of several portions by half during landscaping work in 2001, putting it beyond use. *Photo by Alan R. Smith*

▶ Peter Collins runs high on the banking in his Ferrari-Lancia at Monza during the 1956 Italian Grand Prix. The cars reach peak speeds of over 170 miles per hour and Stirling Moss will beat his previous lap record during the race, circulating in 2 minutes 45.5 seconds—an average of 135.4 miles per hour. Collins is racing under the ever-present threat of a catastrophic tire failure—his car has already thrown a tread during practice—owing to the nature of the circuit. Peter Garnier will write in *The Autocar*, "The banking on the high-speed circuit is so bumpy that the drivers are all but thrown out." *Photo by Yves Debraine*

STIRLING MOSS

All of us went a little deaf. I'm quite fortunate in that my hearing isn't too bad. Earplugs didn't exist and the helmets didn't cover your ears. Everything whistled by so quickly. But I can't complain; I loved driving fast and I enjoyed the sensation of speed for its own sake. The matter of being exposed in the car didn't come into it, because they were all like that.

STIRLING MOSS

There's a very fine line between bravery and stupidity. They're almost the same thing. Sometimes they *are* the same thing. But if you're going so fast that you're frightening yourself, then you're going too fast.

Nevertheless, the element of danger was appealing. I was very young. One of the reasons I raced was that it was dangerous. It was an important ingredient. It was what spiced it up. You could control the amount of fear you had; nobody was pushing your foot down but yourself. My father said at the beginning, "You've got to wear a crash hat." I remember saying to him, "But, Dad, that's a bit sissy." None of the fast drivers did it—[Louis] Chiron, [Jean-Pierre] Wimille, they were all wearing cloth helmets. Still, he insisted, so I wore one.

◀ Speed is king at the 1958 French Grand Prix Reims: The cars exceed 155 miles per hour on the straights and the organizers reward drivers averaging over 130 miles per hour in practice with 100 bottles of champagne. Stirling Moss (8), Juan Manuel Fangio (34), and Harry Schell (16) do their best for Vanwall, Maserati, and BRM, but the grunt of the Ferrari Dino 246 means that Mike Hawthorn leaves with the win—and, thanks to the various prize bonuses on offer, 300 bottles of bubbly. *Photo by Yves Debraine*

▶ Jack Brabham swoops around Tabac during the 1959 Monaco Grand Prix. Stirling Moss looks almost untouchable in the lead until his transmission fails, by which time Brabham has pedaled his little Cooper to a new lap record of 1 minute 40.4 seconds, an average of 70 miles per hour. *Photo by Yves Debraine*

JOHN SURTEES

In 1957 I was touching 180 miles per hour on a bike, down the back at Spa-Francorchamps. The cars were going at similar speeds, but for me there was slightly more tension in the cockpit because I didn't have the experience in car racing.

JACK BRABHAM

I found it thrilling to be traveling at racing speed and cornering at the limit.

▲ Ricardo Rodriguez, running third in the 1961 Italian Grand Prix for Ferrari, steals a glance over his shoulder to see if teammate Giancarlo Baghetti is gaining on him. *Photo by Yves Debraine*

◀ Running the 1959 German Grand Prix at Avus does not meet with universal approval. "To hold the German Grand Prix on such a circuit when for years it has been held on the wonderful Nürburgring seems idiotic," writes *Motor Sport's* Denis Jenkinson. The cars reach 120 miles per hour on the steep brick banking before joining a straight stretch of autobahn ending in a hairpin, then return to the banking via the other carriageway of the autobahn. It may not be as evocative as other German circuits, but its West Berlin location ensures a huge crowd. *Photo by Edward Eves*

STIRLING MOSS

I didn't like the 1,500cc era because those little engines weren't powerful enough. The acceleration was less thrilling, and you had to conserve momentum in the corners. I hadn't liked the previous 1,500cc era, either.

Limiting F1 to 1,500cc unsupercharged engines was ridiculous because they were so underpowered and far less satisfying to drive. When it came in, everyone was against it. They kept changing the formula if they thought things were getting too quick. Nowadays they just add chicanes . . .

JACK BRABHAM

1961 was disastrous for Cooper because they changed the engine formula. The 1,500cc formula wasn't very good for us. We had three or four years of struggling because we just didn't have the engine to do it with. You still had a sensation of speed, but the cars didn't feel as quick as before. It wasn't quite so exciting. That's how we ended up going to Indianapolis.

JACKIE STEWART

It wasn't a great deal slower than it is today. Where they're doing 200 miles per hour now, we were doing about 180 miles per hour by the late 1960s. The aerodynamics weren't sophisticated, so we could slipstream really well. Once you got into the draft of another car you could really make use of it. You could feel the difference through the car.

◄ Having arrived at the unloved Le Mans Bugatti circuit for the 1967 French Grand Prix expecting to race Reg Parnell's privateer 2.1-liter V-8 BRM, Chris Irwin finds himself at the wheel of one of the works BRM H-16s. His mistake? Going quicker in the V-8 than either of the two works cars could manage on the first day of practice. Innes Ireland relates the saga in his *Autocar* report: "Having done this, Irwin was a little slow off the mark, and should have hidden the car away until race day. Just as he was about to get into it on the second day of training, the works team said they wanted it for [Jackie] Stewart. And so the usual change round started and Irwin was given the H-16. He was not at all pleased about this and was in two minds about whether or not he would accept the invitation from the Ferrari team manager—no less—to drive their second car." Irwin will run in fourth and be classified fifth after the H-16 breaks an oil line, but his promising career will be cut short when he is seriously injured in a crash at the Nürburgring in 1968. *Photo by Yves Debraine*

► Piers Courage flies the flag for privateers at the 1969 French Grand Prix in a Brabham BT26 entered by Frank Williams. He will be forced out when his nosecone works loose, followed by some of the cockpit bodywork, which interferes with his ability to change gear. *Photo by Yves Debraine*

JACKIE STEWART

I'm deaf today because of my [skeet] shooting
and my racing. In those days, with the open-
face helmets, once you were at racing speed the
buffeting and the noise damaged your ears. We
didn't use earplugs—they weren't around.

CHAPTER 7

CONCENTRATION

"It's very difficult to maintain maximum effort for very long.
There's concentration, then there's physical tiredness,
and mental tiredness that creeps in."

–GRAHAM HILL

◀ The expression on Giuseppe Farina's face captures the full uncertainty of whether the meager drum brakes on the Alfa 158 will actually generate enough braking force to counteract the supercharged straight-eight engine's mighty shove. His efforts to keep the car on the road in this race—the 1950 non-championship Grand Prix des Nations in Geneva—are ultimately frustrated by teammate Luigi Villoresi, who crashes into the crowd and is thrown from his car into the road, causing Farina to spin off while taking evasive action. *Photo by Louis Klemantaski*

Entire books have been committed to print about the phenomenon of being "in the zone." But what does it really mean in practice? For a Formula 1 driver it is the ability to exclude any extraneous outside stimuli and arrive at a state of total concentration on the job in hand.

It is a highly personal process and individual drivers have different ways of articulating their own methods of achieving that state. Some describe it as a means of almost slowing down time; others have said that when they are at the peak of their abilities the process of driving quickly becomes automatic, freeing up their awareness to focus on race strategy.

Drivers of the era had even more to think about: longer races, more fragile cars, and the proximity of hazards that would not be accepted in the modern era. At Reims one year a local resident drove on to the circuit by mistake, heading on a collision course with the race cars.

The tracks' boundary walls were closer than they should be, but it was the same for everyone: and if those walls had to be shaved, kissed or delicately brushed in the name of a fast lap time, then it had to be done. Small wonder, then, that with so many variables it was not always possible to be at ten-tenths for every lap of a three-hour Grand Prix, and that the drivers were not afraid to admit that, even for them, there were limits.

◀ Louis Rosier hustles his Talbot-Lago around Zandvoort in the 1950 non-championship Dutch Grand Prix. He is on something of a roll, having won the Le Mans 24 Hours (co-driving with his son) a month before, and will capitalize on a pit fire for José Froilán González to take the lead—holding off late charges from the Ferraris of Luigi Villoresi and Alberto Ascari to take the win. "His pit staff hung out signals calling for more speed," writes TG Moore in *Motor Sport,* "but Rosier refused to be flurried." *Photo by Louis Klemantaski*

▶ Alberto Ascari is remarkably composed as he races through Raidillon, the fast uphill exit from Eau Rouge, at Spa-Francorchamps in 1952. Having set an average speed of 114 miles per hour during practice, Ascari leads from pole and fends off a challenge from team-mate Giuseppe Farina to win the race, beginning the process of asserting himself as Ferrari team leader. *Photo by Louis Klemantaski*

◀ Stirling Moss shows early promise at the wheel of the HWM-Alta at Bremgarten. The 1952 Swiss Grand Prix is the first of the World Championship season, and run to Formula 2 regulations because insufficient competitive F1 cars exist to make a full grid. Moss gets off to a remarkable start from the fourth row of the grid to run as high as third, behind the Ferraris of Giuseppe Farina and Piero Taruffi, before pitting when his engine starts to misfire. Team owner John Heath withdraws Moss's car, and that of Lance Macklin, on lap 24 after Peter Collins and George Abecassis suffer identical hub failures and crash out. *Photo by Yves Debraine*

STIRLING MOSS

The world championship races were a minimum of three hours. When you raced every week, you developed the stamina to cope with it. I never did anything to keep fit; I didn't need to train. Practice is different from training. I was driving—racing—for at least three days a week; more, if you included testing. So I was in a car for 250-odd days a year.

Even so, it was very demanding, particularly if you didn't adopt a more relaxed driving style. If you were tense, then you were rougher with the car and would suffer more fatigue.

◀ Stirling Moss guides his Mercedes-Benz W196 around Monaco in 1955, face grimy with dust even though this short-wheelbase version of the car has outboard rather than inboard drum brakes. *Photo by Yves Debraine*

▲ Held a week after the 1957 French Grand Prix at Rouen-les-Essarts, the non-championship Grand Prix de Reims attracts a full entry from the factory F1 teams. Here Ferrari's Luigi Musso focuses as he pursues the leading Vanwall of Stuart Lewis-Evans; he will overhaul the young Englishman to win, but has to tackle the final two laps without a clutch after the pedal breaks off. *Photo by Louis Klemantaski*

▲ Jack Brabham's face is a mask of concentration as he guides his Cooper through the daunting Eau Rouge corner at Spa-Francorchamps in 1960. Even though the bridge is not quite at the bottom of the hill, Brabham's suspension is at full compression and likely to be unforgiving of any bumps or deviations as he aims for the second apex. Klemantaski is taking his life in his hands, shooting from the opposite side of the bridge, precisely where anyone missing the first apex is likely to end up. *Photo by Louis Klemantaski*

A provincial bus strike prevents many spectators from attending the 1957 British Grand Prix at Aintree—causing them to miss Stirling Moss taking a much-lauded home win for Vanwall. The teams and drivers are feeling the physical strain of racing for three weekends in a row (there was a non-championship F1 race at Reims between the French and British Grands Prix): Maserati's mechanics complain that fatigue is preventing them from preparing the cars properly and Juan Manuel Fangio is suffering with a gastric complaint. This sequence of pictures taken at the same corner captures the drivers' differing approaches; with £200 on offer to the first driver to lap in under two minutes, each had an incentive to push hard. *Photos by Louis Klemantaski*

STIRLINGMOSS

MIKEHAWTHORN

TONYBROOKS

LUIGIMUSSO

JACK**BRABHAM**   JUAN*MANUEL*FANGIO

HARRY**SCHELL**   PETER**COLLINS**

◀ Dan Gurney holds a handkerchief to his face to prevent his mouth drying out during the 1961 French Grand Prix at Reims. "For the three practice days, the temperature rose steadily from uncomfortably warm to too-hot-to-endure," writes Peter Garnier in *The Autocar*, "while the flat, featureless countryside shimmered and baked under a cloudless sky and blazing sun. The cars became too hot to touch." Neither Gurney nor his Porsche wilt in the conditions, though, and he will swap the lead with Ferrari's Giancarlo Baghetti until the very last lap. *Photo by Günther Molter*

▶ Driving the new V-8–engined BRM with its distinctive "stackpipe" exhausts, Graham Hill is measured and precise as he reels off the laps in the lead of the 1962 Monaco Grand Prix. He is 24 seconds ahead of Bruce McLaren's Cooper and still utterly in control of the race when his engine starts to misfire with 10 laps still to run. *Photo by Yves Debraine*

◀ Phil Hill takes a drink as he accelerates out of Thillois toward the main straight during the 1961 French Grand Prix. Later in the race the surface at this corner will start to melt in the stifling conditions. Disoriented by the heat, Hill stalls his Ferrari and then attempts to push-start it—forgetting that this is against the rules. *Photo by Günther Molter*

GRAHAM HILL

Each person has his own standard of driving and his own limit. Now what I call ten-tenths might not necessarily be what somebody else calls ten-tenths, but to me it's the absolute limit for the car and myself, and it can't be kept up for more than a lap.

You can get in a fast practice lap, for instance, when you're really fighting to get on to the front row or get pole position. You can probably pull out one lap at what I call ten-tenths—100 percent effort. Obviously that's how you get a fastest lap. Sometimes you get three fastest laps, but they're not usually consecutive. It's one lap when you've done everything as near perfect as is possible with the car you've got.

You can't run a full GP at this pace; if you could, every lap would be the same speed and they'd all be fastest laps. It just doesn't happen that way. Most races are run at between eight- and nine-tenths, nine-tenths being a very, very strong pressure—a very, very hard race. Eight-tenths is just a bit less, like when you've got a lead of perhaps 20 seconds.

It's very difficult to maintain maximum effort for very long. There's concentration, then there's physical tiredness, and mental tiredness that creeps in. If you measured effort in a race, you would probably find that it goes in waves—in a long race you might fall off slightly, then come up again. With more experienced drivers this happens less. If it's a particularly hot day you can also suffer from heat exhaustion, and then you get all sorts of funny effects.

▶ Jim Clark rounds the Station Hairpin at Monaco in 1964. He will have much to contend with in this race: his rear anti-roll bar (seen here intact) breaks while he is leading the race, although such are his powers that he is able to continue at unabated pace—while team boss Colin Chapman persuades race director Louis Chiron not to black-flag him. Pitting to have the errant component replaced will cost him two places and he will halt when his oil pressure falls to zero, consoled only by the crowd's enthusiastic cheers as he walks back to the pits. *Photo by Colin Waldeck*

JACKIE STEWART

There was a lot of heat in the cockpit. We didn't have the quality of insulation. Even though the cars were smaller, lighter, less powerful, I would lose a minimum of three kilos during a grand prix. I had to stay fit to be able to sustain my concentration for a full race distance.

◀ John Surtees rounds the Tarzan corner at Zandvoort in his Ferrari 158/63 during the 1964 Dutch Grand Prix. Ahead, World Champion Jim Clark is unassailable in the Lotus, and by the end of the race Surtees is the only driver left unlapped. *Photo by Robert Daley*

▶ On the tricky Clermont-Ferrand circuit, Jackie Stewart squints with concentration as he tries to keep up with ultimate victor Jim Clark. 1965 is Stewart's first season in F1, and *The Autocar* notes that he "seems to star on difficult and strange circuits." *Photo by Yves Debraine*

BRUCE McLAREN

When you're out in a GP car you haven't got time to think about the fact that you're moving fast. You're concentrating on keeping the movement of the car as smooth and graceful as possible, getting the throttle opened just that fraction quicker than last time, and keeping it open all the way when you get there.

At Silverstone you concentrate on shaving the brick walls on the inside, not just an inch or two away, and you hold the car in a drift that if it were any faster would take you into a bank or onto the grass. If you are any slower you know that you're not going to be up with those first three or four. You know perfectly well you are trying just as hard as you possibly can, and I know when I've done a few laps like this, I come in and think to myself, "Well, if anyone tries harder than that, good luck to them."

▲ Bruce McLaren turns in to the Parabolica in his immaculately prepared M7C at Monza in 1969—a hairy corner when running without wings. For the race, McLaren will revert to running small front and rear wings, and comes fourth in an extraordinarily close finish in which the first four cars are separated by just 0.18 seconds. *Photo by Nigel Snowdon*

▶ Encouraged by the Ferrari pit board's exhortation to go faster, Lorenzo Bandini attacks the lap record in pursuit of Jackie Stewart's BRM during the final laps of the 1966 Monaco Grand Prix. He will break it three times, setting his fastest time of 1 minute 29.8 seconds (78.3 miles per hour) on lap 90, but it is not enough to topple Stewart. *Photo by Robert Daley*

"I was put on a stretcher and left on the floor, which was covered in cigarette ends. All the skin was coming off my body."

–JACKIE STEWART

◀ Convinced that his Lotus has simply run one of its fuel tanks dry during the 1960 Monaco Grand Prix, Innes Ireland pushes the car uphill from Beau Rivage in the hope that he can get it going again on the other side. "If I had known how steep the hill was, I would never have tried it," he will write in his autobiography. "There I was, like a half-wit, pushing my guts out to get the car to the top; when I finally got there I was absolutely on my knees . . . I could only push the Lotus a couple of yards at a time, then I'd almost have to lie down under the back wheel to stop the thing rolling back down again." Unfortunately for Ireland, it is his transmission that has broken, and the car will not start again. *Photo by Louis Klemantaski*

An ever-present risk in motor sport is that for one or more competitors the race will come to a premature conclusion, either through faulty machinery or a collision. When racing cars touch one another at speed, the forces that are unleashed are terrifyingly unpredictable. In the 1950s and 1960s, these violent tangential bursts of kinetic energy meant blood, pain, and death.

Often they were solo accidents, caused by "mechanical failure." This bland euphemism remains in use to the modern day and usually describes an occurrence that in itself is utterly humdrum: the breakage of a cross-threaded nut, or a connecting clip that cost at best a few cents. The consequences, in cars that were traveling at up to 180 miles per hour, were catastrophic as the energies dissipated along random trajectories. Often the drivers were not the only casualties, as at the 1961 Italian Grand Prix when 14 spectators lost their lives in the accident that also claimed Ferrari's Wolfgang von Trips.

The drivers bore these risks with quiet stoicism, although many would inwardly prefer that any mechanical malady would manifest itself undramatically, enabling them to coast to a halt, leave their car in the care of the marshals, and stroll back to the pits. When they spoke out—such as when Jackie Stewart began his campaign to improve circuit safety standards—they were often pilloried and accused of cowardice. Such was the code of masculinity in the age . . .

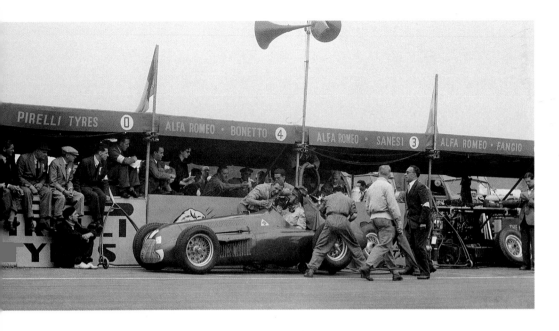

Drivers of the era prefer not to go through the time-consuming ordeal of pit stops, but horsepower gains have rendered them necessary, thanks to the hopped-up engines' prodigious thirst and the stress on rear tires. The stop has yet to become an artfully drilled procedure, as illustrated by this sequence from the 1951 British Grand Prix at Silverstone. Giuseppe Farina has time to take a drink while his mechanics refuel and struggle with the rear tires of his Alfa Romeo 159. The engine then has to be hand-cranked before it will start, enabling Farina to be on his way again. The entire stop costs him 3 minutes 32 seconds. He is destined to retire on lap 75 of 90 with what is officially noted as clutch failure, although contemporary observers note flames shooting out of the car's hood. *Photos by Louis Klemantaski*

STIRLING MOSS

I won every 1.56 races I finished in, but I didn't finish that many races. In racing you're putting everything at the limit—yourself, the car, the wheels, the suspension parts—and because at that time very few of the parts were custom-made for racing, all sorts of things could go wrong. So many of the accidents or retirements in racing were caused by mechanical failure. You had to have great concentration to be able to drive fast and not be troubled by nagging doubts that something may fall off.

▲ José Froilán González communicates his frustration to the Ferrari mechanics after his engine fails on the first lap of the 1954 Belgian Grand Prix at Spa-Francorchamps. An official holds up three fingers to signify that only three people are allowed to work on the car at once, but he is ignored in the commotion. The engine has broken a piston and will take no further part in the race, though González will finish fourth after relieving Mike Hawthorn when the "Farnham Flyer" is overcome by fumes from a leaking exhaust at half distance. *Photo by Louis Klemantaski*

A minor drama unfolds in the Ferrari pit in the closing laps of the 1956 British Grand Prix. Eugenio Castellotti spins at Club, severely damaging his car, and after limping round the course for two laps brings the crippled Ferrari in to the pits. Alfonso de Portago, who has already given his car to Peter Collins, takes over after mechanics replace a buckled wheel. The car is crabbing badly but still has every chance of finishing sixth, although De Portago manages just three more laps before being black-flagged by the stewards. After a long debate he leaves the pits again and does one more slow lap before stopping at the finishing line, pushing the car over as Juan Manuel Fangio takes the checkered flag.

▲ Castellotti is prevailed upon to get out of the car. *Photo by Alan R. Smith*

▲ De Portago jumps in as Castellotti disconsolately removes his helmet. Juan Manuel Fangio's girlfriend, Donna Andrea, nicknamed "Fangina," is standing behind the pit wall at left. *Photo by Alan R. Smith*

▲ Andrea commiserates with the frustrated Castellotti, while race officials look on. *Photo by Louis Klemantaski*

▲ After persuading the stewards to allow him to continue and essaying one final, slow lap, de Portago pushes the battered Ferrari over the line for an eventual classification of 10th. *Photo by Louis Klemantaski*

This sequence of photos highlights the chaotic nature of pit stops at the time, as mechanics, race officials, spectators, and even Donna Andrea (right) are allowed access to the pit box. Juan Manuel Fangio brings his Maserati 250F to a halt on lap 41—just before half distance—of the 1957 Italian Grand Prix. Due to the high speeds attained on the Monza circuit, Pirelli are unable to guarantee the longevity of the tires over a full race distance, and the stop will cost Fangio—who was already nearly 18 seconds behind Stirling Moss's Vanwall—almost a full lap. The gap will enable Moss to make a precautionary pit stop of his own for an oil top-up and a new rear tire; yet second place is enough for Fangio to clinch the World Championship. *Photos by Louis Klemantaski*

JACKIE STEWART

It was dangerous. People were dying. The penalties were high, but so were the benefits, because serious money was arriving in the sport. In 1969 I'd have been making a million pounds a year. That was a lot of money back then; the chairman of ICI would have been making around £15,000.

But nobody wanted to talk about the risks. Many people thought that we were like gladiators. It was big money, so people would say, "Well, he's getting paid a lot, so if he doesn't like it he should go and do something else. If the kitchen's too hot, get out." I never looked at it like that. I never thought I was being paid for bravery; I thought I was being paid for my skills. I didn't think we should be dying unnecessarily when the racetracks could be improved.

There were no barriers or run-off areas. The cars had no seat belts. There were trees, telegraph poles, and even marshals' posts in the way—Bruce McLaren died because he hit a marshals' post which shouldn't have been there. The medical facilities were pathetic. The chief medical officer at one racetrack was a gynecologist—not an orthopedic man, not an internal medicine man, not a burns man, not a brain surgeon. These things needed to be changed.

◄ Jackie Stewart has to complete the final laps of the 1967 Belgian Grand Prix steering with one hand while holding the gearlever in place with the other. In this picture he is trying to relieve his cramped wrist. Having taken the lead after Jim Clark pitted to have a broken spark plug changed, Jackie Stewart is set for victory in the recalcitrant H-16–engined BRM . . . until gearbox problems intervene. Dan Gurney roars past to notch up a maiden win for his Eagle marque. *Photo by Nigel Snowdon*

STIRLING MOSS

I had lots of accidents through mechanical failure—seven times I had a wheel come off and I had eight brake failures. A couple of times I had the steering shear; I was turning a corner and my arms just crossed over. I don't know how many times I got hit by another car, or tires blew.

▲ A bad day for Ferrari on the Monaco harbor front in 1957: On the fourth lap, the Vanwall of race leader Stirling Moss experiences brake failure at the chicane, sending car and driver into the hay bales. Peter Collins swerves his Ferrari (26) to avoid Moss and hits the wall, while teammate Mike Hawthorn (28) is unsighted and rams into the rear of the other Vanwall, driven by Tony Brooks. The stricken Ferraris remain there for the duration. Having threaded his Maserati through the initial chaos, Juan Manuel Fangio (32) goes on to win. *Photo by Louis Klemantaski*

FRANK WILLIAMS

I never yearn for the good old days. The business of sliding around—it wasn't as dramatic as that. The cars were unsafe; if you had a big accident you would do yourself a mischief.

▲ Little recognizable is left of Mike Taylor's Lotus after a violent high-speed accident during practice for the 1960 Belgian Grand Prix. Taylor has survived the impact—his steering column snapped while he was running flat-out at the La Carriere corner and the car knocked down trees as it left the circuit, ending up so far out of sight that his absence was not noticed until the end of the session—but his injuries are so severe that he will never race again. *Photo by Yves Debraine*

JACKIE STEWART

When something like that happens, you're in the hands of the gods. At Spa-Francorchamps in 1966 there had been a sudden downpour after the start. I was coming into the Masta Kink at 170 miles per hour when the car went over a river of water on the track surface. It aquaplaned and I lost control. It was like being strapped to a missile. There were fences, trees, a woodcutter's hut that I knocked down, a telegraph pole—I was lucky to survive. Graham Hill hit the same patch of water but just spun around and ended up facing the right direction to carry on. He was about to do that when he saw me and what was left of my car.

I don't remember the moment of impact. I remember being in the car, trapped. And although I don't remember being removed from the car, I remember immediately afterward. I was lying in a hay truck. There were no marshals. Graham Hill and Bob Bondurant had stopped to help. Bob had to run across the track and borrow a spanner from some spectators because the steering wheel was trapping me in the wreckage. They took my overalls off because I was soaked in fuel and my skin was burning.

I remember being taken to the so-called medical center in the pit area, by the tower. I was put on a stretcher and left on the floor, which was covered in cigarette ends. All the skin was coming off my body.

Then I was in an ambulance with [my wife] Helen, [BRM spokesman] Louis Stanley, and Jim Clark. I was starting to groan with the pain, and Jimmy just leaned over and said, "For goodness sake, pull yourself together—Helen's here."

◄ The aftermath of the first-lap pile-up at the 1966 Belgian Grand Prix at Spa-Francorchamps. *Opposite top:* Jo Bonnier's Cooper-Maserati (20) is left dangling precariously over a steep drop. *Opposite bottom:* The shattered remains of Jackie Stewart's BRM (15). *Left:* American Bob Bondurant's BRM (24). *Photos by Ami Guichard*

JACK BRABHAM

A lot of the circuits we went to . . . you look back now, and we were really risking our necks. The road circuits had trees, rock gardens in the middle of the road, even tramlines. There were so many obstacles you could kill yourself with.

FRANK WILLIAMS

The drivers knew their lives were at risk every time they went out. It sounds romantic, but it wasn't. People died. It wasn't dinner conversation, really.

◀ When the high-level wing on Graham Hill's Lotus 49B fails at speed at Montjuich Park during the 1969 Spanish Grand Prix there is nothing he can do to prevent an enormous accident. He emerges unscathed, but, owing to the nature of the track, the remnants of his car cannot be cleared. Ten laps later, at the same spot, his teammate Jochen Rindt suffers an identical failure. "The hump of the hill exaggerated the loss of the downward forces of the wing," Innes Ireland writes in his *Autocar* report. "There was absolutely nothing Rindt could do, and the car almost flew through the air into the guard rail. It started to run up the rails, the right-front wheel being completely clear of the top rail at one point, then came down and smashed heavily into the wreckage of Hill's car." This is one of several incidents that moves Rindt to consider switching to the Brabham team for 1970. *Photo by Nigel Snowdon*

▲ Dan Gurney races through to second place in the 1961 Italian Grand Prix. In all, he will pass this scene—just before the Parabolica, where the Ferrari of Wolfgang von Trips (4) plowed off the circuit, killing Von Trips and 14 spectators—42 times before the end of the race. The Lotus of Jim Clark is also visible in the ditch on the left. Despite the calamitous turn of events, spectators are still permitted to stand in an area where so many of their number had been mown down.
Photo by Robert Daley

Beyond the immediate dangers of high-speed impacts, the specter of fire always looms in the aftermath of a crash. On lap 37 of the 1955 International Trophy at Silverstone, Ken Wharton tries to overtake Roy Salvadori's Maserati at Club; Wharton's Vanwall slides onto the grass and hits a concrete corner marker, which breaks the rear axle and pierces the fuel tank. The car instantly catches fire and burns fiercely. Wharton, badly burned and disoriented, staggers into the middle of the track before collapsing on the grass. It is a miraculous escape. *Photo by Louis Klemantaski*

Jo Schlesser's Honda RA302 burns uncontrollably after crashing in the opening laps of the 1968 French Grand Prix at Rouen-les-Essarts. The car is an experimental magnesium-bodied monocoque chassis with inboard front springs and an air-cooled V-8. The car is compact and wind-cheating, but undeveloped—which is why John Surtees declined to race it, opting to use his RA301. With Soichiro Honda himself in the area on a sales push, the company has elected to enter the car anyway under the Honda France banner, and recruited Schlesser to drive. After an absurdly long program of supporting events the race gets away, in light drizzle, at 4:30 p.m. On the third lap Schlesser's car spins on the wet surface and runs up a bank, exploding with terrifying ferocity before overturning, trapping the doomed Schlesser inside. It takes 20 minutes to bring the fire under control. Inexplicably, the race continues, and for lap after lap the cars pick their way past the burning wreckage. *Photo by Nigel Snowdon*

STIRLING MOSS

I never wore a seat belt because of the danger of fire. The cars could carry up to 53 gallons of fuel, and some of it was pretty volatile stuff. In the 1950s, there were all sorts of chemical additives in it to boost the octane. We even used aviation fuel. If you crashed and then got trapped in the car when that lot went up, you were done for.

STIRLING MOSS

You knew there was a danger of death, but you also knew that thinking about it wasn't going to make it any less likely to happen. Besides, I wouldn't have wanted to drive a racing car unless there was some sort of danger involved. For me, risk was a very necessary ingredient.

▲ Chris Amon, driving in his first grand prix for Ferrari, witnesses the dreadful accident that claims the life of teammate Lorenzo Bandini. "I think it was sheer fatigue," Amon will say in his biography. "It was a long race, the thick end of three hours, and it was very hot that day. I know by the 75th lap I was actually starting to get cold in the car, which meant that I was totally dehydrated. I'm sure he went through the same thing and it was purely a lapse of concentration that caused him to run wide and hit the bales." *Photo by Robert Daley*

CHAPTER 9

THE FINISH

"I'm never 100 percent satisfied that I've done a perfect job, because you can never be perfect."

–GRAHAM HILL

◄ The ever-colorful Louis Chiron shows 1966 winner Jackie Stewart the checkered flag with his usual theatrical flourish. *Photo by Nigel Snowdon*

You would imagine that crossing the finishing line would unleash a torrent of emotions: joy in victory, relief in survival, despair in defeat. Often, though, racers confess to being too preoccupied with the actual business of racing—beating the man ahead, managing the technical vagaries of the machinery, concentrating on not making mistakes—to properly enjoy a victory in the heat of the moment. The race was everything to them; its end left them in an emotional vacuum, a curious hinterland of semi-satisfaction, like reaching the top of a mountain only to find nothing of consequence there—or that a neighboring peak was slightly higher.

The ritual of winning was much shorter than in modern F1. Before podium ceremonies became regimented to the second to satisfy global TV schedules, a driver could slip off with his garland and champagne and perhaps seek to parlay his moment of glory into some success with the local womenfolk. He would certainly not have to utter sponsor-friendly platitudes to the waiting microphones of the world's press.

Nor, too, was there much satisfaction to be had in being the gallant loser, elevating an underperforming car to a finishing position it scarcely deserved.

Whatever a racer's finishing position, his focus inevitably turned to the next event . . . At all times their judgment was colored by the practicalities of getting to the following race, of securing that next hit.

GRAHAM HILL

You never know that you *won't* win a race. I never accept that I'm *not* going to win a race. I never even think about the possibility that I'm not going to win—I always go out to try to win. I know that sometimes I might win only by default, but I'm still out there trying to win, and I think the moment any driver accepts that he's not going to win the race, it's a little chink in his armor. The will to win is terribly important to a racing driver.

Contrasting styles of checkered flag presentation. *Opposite:* Alberto Ascari receives a stiffly formal greeting after completing a torrid 1952 Belgian GP. *Above:* Joy unbridled as home hero Stirling Moss wins the 1957 British Grand Prix in a British car. *Photos by Louis Klemantaski*

◀ In this sequence of photos, the race is not quite finished yet, but the inimitable Jean Behra has nearly called it a day. Having pitted for a new wheel and to complain to the Maserati team about his down-on-power engine, he comes to a complete halt within sight of the finishing line of the 1957 French Grand Prix at Rouen-les-Essarts. His trousers are covered with lubricant from a burst oil radiator, which has also deposited much of its contents on the track. After chatting with Carlos Menditéguy (top left), and with ten minutes of the race left to run, Behra takes a drink (top right) before pushing his car across the line as the checkered flag waves for the winner, Juan Manuel Fangio (bottom). Behra believes that this is enough for him to hold on to the fifth place he was running in before the breakdown, but the organizers refuse to credit him for his final lap and award the position to Harry Schell. The result leaves Behra equal second in the drivers' standings with Ferrari's Luigi Musso on seven points, but Fangio is well clear on 25. Photos by Edward Eves

▶ Jackie Stewart crosses the line without fanfare after a bitterly disappointing race. Thanks to a minor error in calculating his gas mileage—team boss Ken Tyrrell thought it would be 7 miles per gallon but it was closer to 6.6—Stewart ran out of fuel on the last lap, losing the lead to Bruce McLaren. Nevertheless it is a remarkable performance by Stewart, who is racing with his injured wrist in a protective brace that affords very little movement. Photo by Nigel Snowdon

Sealed with a kiss: José Froilán González gets an unexpected reward after ending Alfa Romeo's dominance with his remarkable victory for Ferrari in the 1951 British Grand Prix. *Photo by Louis Klemantaski*

STIRLING MOSS

If a race win simply fell into my lap, I wouldn't find it very satisfactory unless I'd absolutely worked for it. My ethos was that I'd rather lose a race driving fast enough to win it than win a race driving slowly enough to lose it. Jackie Stewart, Alain Prost, and so on—they've been very successful and achieved incredible things, but in a very different way from my approach.

▲ Stirling Moss deserves the plaudits after triumphing in a tense and exciting 1956 Italian Grand Prix at Monza. After a pitched battle with the Ferrari of Juan Manuel Fangio and the Vanwall of Harry Schell, Moss opened a lead of over a minute in his Maserati 250F before running out of fuel. Privateer 250F driver Luigi Piotti then contrived to hit Moss's slowing car from behind, giving it enough impetus to reach the pits. Note the balding rear-left tire, which prompted Maserati to instruct Moss to slow down in the final laps, enabling Fangio to close to within five seconds at the checkered flag. Having clinched the World Championship for Fangio with second place, Ferrari elects not to protest Moss's win. *Photo by Yves Debraine*

◀ Juan Manuel Fangio is mobbed after seizing victory by the narrowest of margins from Ferrari teammate Luigi Musso in the non-championship 1956 Syracuse Grand Prix—a thrilling conclusion to a race which, with only 15 cars on the grid, had promised little. Nevertheless, the presence of Mille Miglia co-founder Renzo Castagneto (holding the checkered flag) indicates the prestige of the event. *Photo by Louis Klemantaski*

STIRLING MOSS

I'd never shaken a bottle of champagne in my life. In my era it just wasn't done! You'd stand on the podium with a garland or something while they took pictures of you, and then you'd go off and chase the crumpet . . . A Grand Prix win was best celebrated with a lady. You looked to the next race, yes, but after a win I found it best to milk the situation as hard as I could . . .

▲ Stirling Moss has parked his victorious privately entered Lotus 18 in front of the royal box at Monaco in 1961. Note how in this more genteel era, before the days of champagne spraying, a beverage is being decanted from a bottle into a cup for him. *Photo by Robert Daley*

JACKIE STEWART

It would take me at least one or two days to come down from what I called the "iceberg position." I never jumped in the air or got emotional after winning a race. I just said, "Thank you very much." When I won the World Championship at Monza in 1969, I was staying at the Villa D'Este at Lake Como; as I was walking down the staircase the morning after, I could hear the concierge trying to get me on to a different flight. He was saying, "But you've got to do this, it's for the world champion, Jackie Stewart." And that's when it hit me. It hadn't occurred to me before then.

◀ After winning the 1969 Italian Grand Prix— and with it, the World Championship—Jackie Stewart looks as impassive as the rest of the crowd are excited. His wife Helen (in the striped scarf) walks alongside as the people in the grandstands begin their traditional circuit invasion. *Photo by Yves Debraine*

JACK BRABHAM

Winning a race gave you the best feeling afterwards. My favorite race was the French Grand Prix in 1960. To beat the Ferraris at Reims, which was such a high-speed and power-dependent circuit, was a fantastic feeling. But the 1960 Belgian Grand Prix at Spa was one I can never forget. There were two other drivers [Chris Bristow and Alan Stacey] killed during that race, which took the shine off winning it, I can assure you.

◄ José Froilán González (left) looks down at his victorious BRM after winning the 15-lap Goodwood Trophy Formula Libre race in September 1952. Reg Parnell (right) and Ken Wharton (sipping from trophy) have made it a 1-2-3 for the troubled Bourne-based marque, but in the absence of serious competition (Giuseppe Farina's Ferrari-based Thin Wall Special failed to start) not everyone is impressed. "For three modern Formula 1 cars to finish a race of just over 36 miles cannot, by any stretch of the imagination, be called an epoch-making event," says *Autosport's* editorial the following week. *Photo by Alan R. Smith*

► Jack Brabham celebrates a remarkable victory in the 1960 French Grand Prix at Reims, having outpaced Ferrari throughout the weekend on what is traditionally a power circuit where Maranello's cars figure well. He was challenged by Phil Hill and Wolfgang von Trips for 28 flat-out laps until the Ferraris withdrew with transmission trouble. *Photo by Ami Guichard*

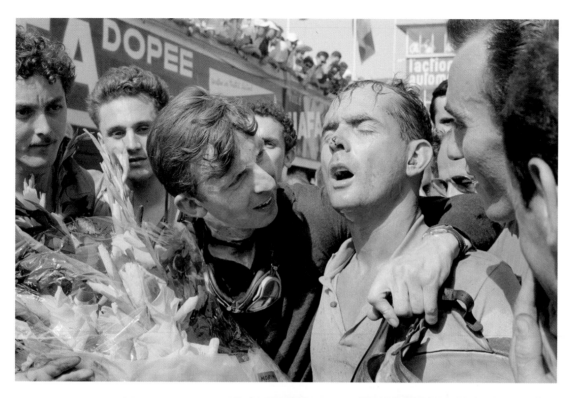

◀ Ferrari's Tony Brooks (left) has won the 1959 French Grand Prix, but teammate Phil Hill's face betrays the physical effort of racing flat out on a day when ground temperatures on the start line reached 130 degrees Fahrenheit (54 degrees Celsius). Hill, who finished second, is not the only driver to suffer from the heat and the flying stones from the ailing track surface. "The scene at the pits when the race was over was indescribable," relates *Motor Sport's* report, "with prostrate drivers everywhere, many of them cut and bleeding from flying stones and molten tar; some lucky enough to be able to relax, others having to recover sufficient energy to start in the F2 race which was due to follow." *Photo by Ami Guichard*

◀ Princess Grace and Prince Rainier are on hand to present Stirling Moss with his trophy after winning the 1960 Monaco Grand Prix. It is something of a tradition for Prince Rainier to essay a quick lap of the circuit before the race in a road car, which this year was a new Peugeot 404. *Photo by Robert Daley*

JACKIE STEWART

Dan Gurney had started the practice of spraying champagne on the podium at the Le Mans 24 Hours. The first time I did it was a total accident. I'd just won the [1969] Dutch GP at Zandvoort. The bottle had been left out in the sun, so the champagne foamed out as soon as I uncorked it. I instinctively put my thumb over the top to try to stop it, but that just made it spray even harder.

◀ Contemporary reports will describe Jim Clark as looking "tired and wet" when he emerges from his car after winning the 1963 Belgian Grand Prix for Lotus. Here he looks composed after 32 flawless laps of Spa-Francorchamps, during which a heavy thunderstorm hit the circuit, prompting several teams to discuss the possibility of asking the organizers to stop the race early. *Photo by Nigel Snowdon*

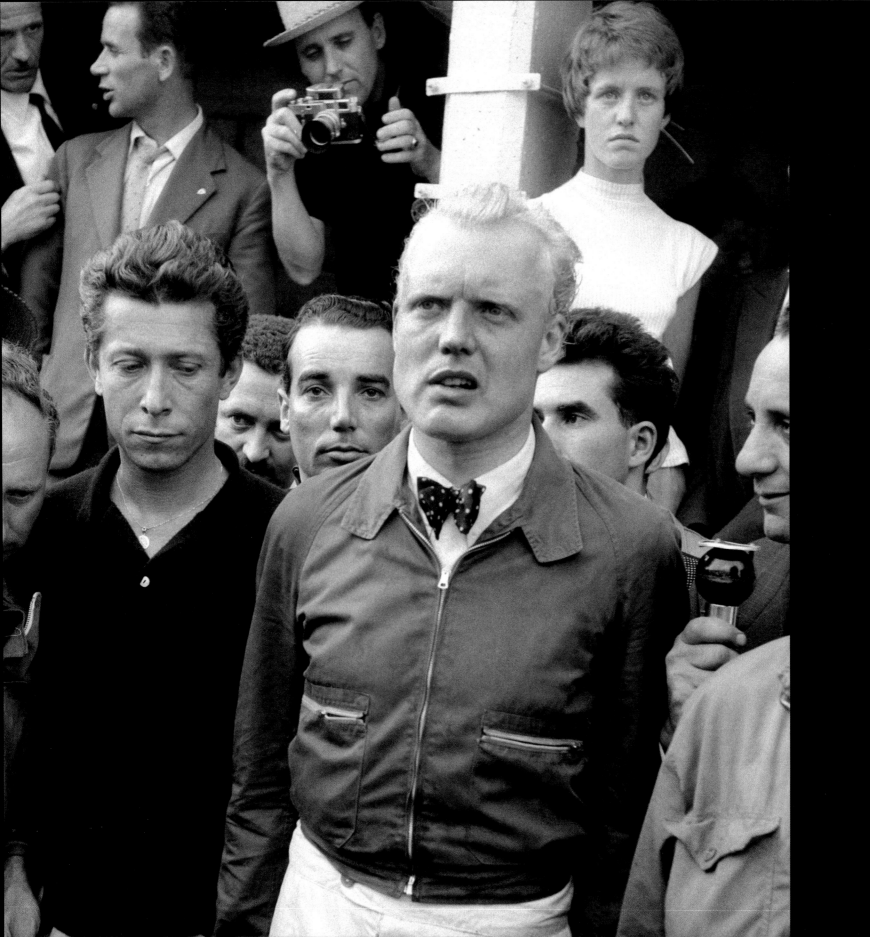

◄ A victory tinged with sadness: Mike Hawthorn (right) has just won the 1958 French Grand Prix for Ferrari from Olivier Gendebien (left, also the victor in the 12-hour sports car race that preceded the GP), but everyone is waiting for news of Luigi Musso, who has been rushed to the hospital after crashing out of the race. Musso's wounds would prove fatal. *Photo by Yves Debraine*

▲ A surreal photo of a surreal scene: Phil Hill has just won the 1961 Italian Grand Prix for Ferrari while gathering enough points to secure the World Championship; but the look on his and Carlo Chiti's faces underline what a bleak victory this is: Hill's teammate Wolfgang von Trips perished in a first-lap accident which also killed 14 spectators. *Photo by Robert Daley*

GRAHAM HILL

In some of what I think have been my best races I might have come only ninth, but I've done it in a car that was a heap or had something wrong with it. If I know that I've done a reasonably good job I'm reasonably happy. Mind you, I'm never 100 percent satisfied that I've done a perfect job, because you can never be perfect. If I know that I haven't really tried too much, if I haven't really put much effort into it through being dispirited because the car isn't going well, I feel I've lost my battle—I've lost my race with myself.

◄ Reg Parnell has good reason to be cheerful after finishing fourth in the Thin Wall Special at Reims in 1951: He has driven a strong race despite the handicap of failing brakes, and his transmission failed just as he approached the finishing line—saving him a long trudge back to the pits on a typically hot Reims summer day. *Photo by Louis Klemantaski*

► Perhaps a drink will help? Ferrari's Giuseppe Farina is thoroughly agitated in the pits after the 1953 Swiss Grand Prix at Bremgarten, and with good reason: Having fought back up to the lead after dropping to seventh place on the opening lap, he had been expecting to coast to victory ahead of teammates Mike Hawthorn and Alberto Ascari. But in defiance of a team order to hold station, Ascari has put on a charge and passed both his teammates to win by over a minute and claim the World Championship for himself. No wonder the atmosphere is somewhat tense. *Photo by Louis Klemantaski*

JOHN SURTEES

It's never satisfying to go along and lose. At times you get a little comfort, but when you lose, the main thing you do is analyze why and make certain it doesn't happen again.

◀ Wolfgang von Trips describes to his Ferrari mechanics what went wrong during the 1957 Monaco Grand Prix: While running third, his engine seized in Casino Square, spinning him into the barriers. "Trips was unhurt, but the barrier as well as the local masonry suffered considerably," reports Peter Garnier in *The Autocar*. *Photo by Louis Klemantaski*

▶ Mike Hawthorn and Stirling Moss—both early retirements—congratulate Tony Brooks on his fine second place in the 1957 Monaco Grand Prix. The soot and brake dust on his face attests to the efforts Brooks has gone to—he is the only other driver to finish on the leading lap with Juan Manuel Fangio, the winner. *Photo by Louis Klemantaski*

Two masters of their respective crafts: Louis Klemantaski *(right)* with Juan Manuel Fangio on the grid before the start of the 1956 British Grand Prix at Silverstone.

AFTERWORD

Louis Klemantaski: An Appreciation

As a photographer of modern day Formula 1, I often look to the lensmen of the past for inspiration, and none more so than possibly the best of the best: Louis Klemantaski. Back in simpler—and, one can imagine, more enjoyable—times in which to photograph motor racing, he set a standard by which all who follow will be judged.

Klemantaski's pit and paddock pictures, although not always striking in their composition or content, still exhibit all the necessary ingredients that make up an interesting shot, encouraging the viewer to look long and hard at the picture in front of them.

When you get to the action shots there is quite a bit more experimentation with angles and motion blur. In this respect he was pushing the boundaries, both of what was technically possible (given the relatively primitive camera technology

and film stock) and of what readers liked and expected. I find it astounding that to this day there are people who prefer a "frozen" shot to a dynamic one with motion blur.

Ansell Adams, the legendary "father of modern day photography" once said: "A good photograph is knowing where to stand," and no one shooting grand prix racing cars has better illustrated that statement than Klemantaski. Standing in the right place is important, but once there it's all about making the location work, and that—in my opinion—is what he did best.

For example, just take a look at some of his studies of cars racing around the streets of Monte Carlo. Klemantaski got more out of the camera, lens, location, and subject matter than 99 per cent of racing car photographers before or since. It's not just on the streets of the famous Principality that he did this. No, at pretty much every track

Klemantaski made the drivers of the day aboard their thoroughbred cars look just that little bit more fearless, faster, and heroic than his fellow photographers did.

I sometimes wonder what a treat it must have been to work trackside when Klemantaski plied his trade on the race tracks of Europe, his creativity unhindered by Armco barriers, sky-high debris fencing, and overly zealous security oafs. As free as he and his fellow photographers were of today's restrictive safety measures, they still had to make the most of the locations available. It was Louis Klemantaski's ability to do this so well that built his formidable reputation, and is why he is regarded by many as the greatest ever exponent of the art of photographing racing cars in motion.

—*Darren Heath, Fall 2010*

PHOTO REFERENCE NUMBERS

The photos in this book* are available for purchase from The Klemantaski Collection, including, in some cases, prints signed by the photographer. Visit www.klemcoll.com for more details. The following are reference numbers for each image:

COVER
Front — 66AG4-24
Back — 57C2J-23A

FRONT MATTER
Page 1 — 61C1-8
2 — 57EJ7-3
8 — 50ASJ-F47

PROLOGUE
10 — C61D9A-4
12 — CYD-P-21A-8
13 — 64D7A-18A
14 — 62M1J-66
15 — 62WJ1-14
16 — 66M1B-4A
17 — 65YD1F-3
18 — 69S019-26A
19 (Amon) — C69YD4B-12
19 (Ascari) — 53YD2B-6
19 (Baghetti) — CYD-P3-4
20 (Bandini) — C65CWA-2
20 (Behra) — 56M5D-18
20 (Bonnier) — CYD-P4-2
21 (Brooks) — 59M1F-34
21 (Castelotti) — CYD-P7-4
21 (Chiron) — 49ASJ-F5
22 (Clark) — 61M2C-87
22 (Collins) — 56C2A-6
22 (Courage) — 68M1B-6A
23 (Fangio) — 57AG13E-9
23 (Farina) — 51ASJ-F95
23 (Gendebien) — 59PC21E-21
24 (Ginther) — 63YD5D-20
24 (González) — 54ASJ-N32
24 (Gregory) — 60E3A-17
25 (Gurney) — C59E1-4
25 (Hawthorn) — 53AG3A-21
25 (P. Hill) — C61D4B-28
26 (Hulme) — 65M1F-37
26 (Ickx) — 68M1B-26A
26 (Ireland) — 62YD4C-20
27 (Lewis-Evans) — 57C6F-11A
27 (Musso) — 56YD9B-29
27 (Rindt) — 66YD3B-20
28 (Rodriguez) — 62PC3-27
28 (Schell) — 57YD3C-12
29 (Siffert) — 62M4B-43
29 (Taruffi) — 52YD1C-5
29 (Trintignant) — CYD-P25-1
29 (von Trips) — C61M8-3

CHAPTER 1
30 — 57EJ5-1
32 — 50R1E-14
34, top — 52C3A-18A
34, bottom — 57PC2A-44
35 — C58PC7A-13
36 — 57C4A-24A
37 — C54MJ-8
38 — 64WJ1-1
39 — 69S065-19
40 — 57C2J-17A
41 — 50R1L-28A
42 — 55C5A-8
43 — 54R20-12
44 — C59PC4B-2
45 — C53M2A-5
46 — 56AG1C-22
47 — 58AG13F-1
48 — 66D1A-21
49, top — 69S144-9
49, bottom —

CHAPTER 2
50 — C54YD3A-4
52 — C55M5-6
54 — 52R6B-9
55 — C54C5-1
56 — 55ASJ-NB51
57 — 55AG1E-24A
58 — C55YD4A-3
59 — 57C2J-23A
60 — 57C4A-11A
62, left — 58E19G-56
62, right — 58EJ20-2
63 — C59PC2A-8
64 — C59PC6B-6
65, left — 60D3B-9
65, right — 60YD3A-16
66 — 64YD3A-11A
67 — 63PC26A-9A
68 — 64D4C-23

69 — 66AG2C-20
70 — 68S092-33A-2891
71 — 67S001-25A

CHAPTER 3
72 — C61AG1-5
74, top — 50ASJ-A3
74, bottom — 64M7F-6
75, top — C57E6-5
75, bottom — C64D4B-2
76, left — 56ASJ-D3
76, right — 58E14G-52
77 — 66D2B-7A
78 — 56C7D-17A
80, left — 53ASJ-M50
80, center — 53ASJ-M13
80, right — 56R2-24
81, left — 56R4-5
81, center — 55ASJ-H6
81, right — 58E11W-77
82, top — 62D7D-2A
82, left — 62D7D-5A
82, center — 62D7D-6A
82, right — 62D7D-7A
83 — 60D4A-31
84 — C61D9C-11
86 — 56ASJ-N75
87 — C61D10-19
88 — 62M3D-26
90, top — 52ASJ-I67
90, bottom — 57R1-59
91 — 63WJ2-9
92 — C65WJ-4
93 — C69YD1A-2
94 — 60M4G-33
95 — C67C1E-2
96, top — 57C4A-30A
96, bottom — 60M1H-40
97 — 58YD1A-16

CHAPTER 4
98 — 53C5D-38A
100 — 51C3A-15
102 — C54YD4-5
103 — 55ASJ-NB61
104 — 56C4F-21

105 — C58YD2B-2
106, top — C58PC7B-15
106, bottom — C58PC7D-16
107, top — C58E11A-6
107, bottom — 58E10K-89
108 — C59YD5A-1
109 — 61M1N-56
110 (Porto) — 60D8B-17
111 (McLaren) — 67S012-18-67270
112 — C55YD4E-1
113 — 56YD5G-35
114 — 56M8A-30A
115 — 61D8-22

CHAPTER 5
116 — C65WJ-11
118 — 51C2-33A
120, top — 54C7D-2A
120, bottom — 54C10D-38
121 — 56C4A-18
122 — 59AG2G-3
123 — 61M2B-11
124, top — 55ASJ-NB56
124, bottom — 55ASJ-NB57
125 — 55R10E-21
126 — 51R5A-37
128 — C57PC2A-2
129 — 57C4D-12
130, top — 58E20J-87
130, bottom — 58YD8D-7
131 — 59M2A-5A
132, top — 60C2A-27A
132, bottom — 64WJ1-5
133, top — 65YD4B-17
133, bottom — 68S040-1198
134, top — 63CW58-33
134, bottom — 63S016-26
135, top — 63WJ2-8
135, bottom — 63WJ2-5
136, top — 55M3L-36
136, bottom — 65YD2E-9
137 — 66AG2A-25

CHAPTER 6
138 — 57C4-16
140 — 55ASJ-NB72

141 — 56YD9B-37
142 — C58YD4A-8
143 — C59YD1-1
144 — C59E1-3
145 — 61YD7A-30
146 — 67YD4D-12
147 — 69YD4C-29A

CHAPTER 7
148 — 50C3D-35
150, top — 50C2A-25
150, bottom — 52YD1C-2
151 — 52C3A-32A
152 — C55YD2B-1
153, top — 57C5C-5
153, bottom — 60C2A-14
154 (Moss) — 57R2D-10A
154 (Hawthorn) — 57R2D-11A
154 (Brooks) — 57R2D-14A
154 (Musso) — 57R2D-15A
155 (Brabham) — 57R2D-19A
155 (Fangio) — 57R2D-24A
155 (Schell) — 57R2D-25A
155 (Collins) — 57R2D-12A
156, top — 61M5E-30
156, bottom — 61M5F-14
157 — C62YD2B-2
158 — C64WJ-3
160 — 64D5B-20
161 — C65YD4A-5
162 — 69S166-16A
163 — 66D1F-32A

CHAPTER 8
164 — C60C1-28
166, top left — 51R5C-9
166, top right — 51R5C-10
166, bottom left — 51R5C-12
166, bottom right — 51R5C-13
167 — 54C5A-29
168, left — 56ASJ-M12
168, right — 56ASJ-M11
169, left — 56R4-84
169, right — 56R4-55
170, top — 57C7C-2A
170, bottom — 57C7C-3A

171 — 57C7C-4A
172 — 67S04-0A-1424
174 — 57C2F-28
175 — 60YD4A-14
176, top — 66AG2A-10
176, bottom — 66AG2D-6A
177 — 66AG2D-9A
178, top — 69S069-6A
178, bottom — 69S069-8A
179 — C61D10-6
180, top — 55R4F-16
180, bottom — 68S064-2063
181 — C67D1A-8

CHAPTER 9
182 — 66S009-0A
184 — 52C3E-22A
185 — 57R2B-22A
186, top left — 57E12H-22
186, top right — 57E12H-23
186, bottom — 57E12H-24
187 — 68S049-1532
188 — 51R5E-30
189 — 56YD9E-31
190 — 56C2D-25
191 — 61D3A-9
192 — 69YD3F-23
194 — 52ASJ-IB72
195 — 60AG8C-33
196, top — 59AG6F-16
196, bottom — 60D3A-35
197 — 63S004-25A
198 — 58YD4B-28
199 — C61D10-2
200 — 51C2D-38A
201 — 53C6C-16
202 — 57C2C-14
203 — 57C2C-18

AFTERWORD
204 — 56R4-4

INDEX
208 — 60PC20C-40

* Excepting those on pages 6 and 205

EVENTS

FORMULA 1 CHAMPIONSHIP RACES

NON-CHAMPIONSHIP RACES

MAKES

PEOPLE